You Can't Drive Your Car to Your Own Funeral

ANN MARIE HANCOCK

Copyright © 2018 Ann Marie Hancock
All rights reserved
First Edition

PAGE PUBLISHING, INC.
New York, NY

First originally published by Page Publishing, Inc. 2018

ISBN 978-1-64138-643-2 (Paperback)
ISBN 978-1-64214-897-8 (Hardcover)
ISBN 978-1-64138-644-9 (Digital)

Printed in the United States of America

To Tommy,
the center of my world, the rock that keeps me focused,
the deepest happiness I've ever known, my dearest
dream come true, my soul mate for forty-eight years,
the love of my life, my husband—the Bear.

Preface

From My Heart to Yours

I have written <u>You Can't Drive Your Car to Your Own Funeral</u> with complete dedication, commitment, and the hope that you will find loving solutions to the stressful challenges of caring for a "difficult" <u>dear one.</u> This is my story, but yours as well. We all have a difficult person in our lives. This creates stress and stress changes the chemical structure of the cells, creating illness and disease. We don't need this! Harvard, Yale, Mayo Clinic, and Vanderbilt concur with doctors Alexander Loyd and Ben Johnson when they tell us over ninety percent of illness and disease is related to stress.

One can only conclude that it is imperative to deal with conflict in a positive, loving way. We need all the tools at our disposal. Most important…we want to send love as we would like to receive it. We need to send out uplifting, healing words; we surely all need them.

If you find this book helpful, spread it around. Paraphrasing Dolly Levi, "Love is like manure…no good unless it's spread."

I wish you all the peace, love, joy, and hope available to each when we seek it regardless of circumstances.

Ann Marie Hancock

Introduction

*I believe that the evidence for God lies primarily
in inner personal experiences.*
—William James

"Every time you hear a bell, an angel gives you a wrinkle." I thought the Comedy Club Hallmark card was funny while reminiscent of the Jimmy Stewart classic, *It's a Wonderful Life*. I bought three to send to close maturing friends.

While I chuckled, I also realized there is a central core of truth that I bypassed. Life is short and full of wrinkles. Suffering and death are two such corrugations that are unavoidable. They are very personal and unique to each individual. They remind us that time is a gift, and to respond productively, we must be sincere, courageous, and have a desire for truth.

Suffering is an opportunity for those seeking a personal relationship with God. Some of the elderly are very aware of this. They know the first prom, football game, homecoming, job, and promotion are memories and behind them. They know we are all on a journey, a short journey back to God. So many of the sick and elderly feel hopeless. One exclaimed to me, "Where did it go?" "I was an Olympic skater, young flexible, and sought-after. Now I need a wheelchair and am losing my eyesight. I feel hopeless and have nothing to look forward to in life." Another said, "I was an international corporate president. I traveled the world, ran seventeen marathons, and women everywhere found me charming. Now I am eaten up with cancer and have no future. What's left for me?"

There, but for the grace of God, go any one of us. Earth's linear journey is quick. In the blink of an eye, it's over, but take heart; God knows what He is about. He never leaves us, always providing another opportunity to seek Him.

For many, an internal search commences in the face of tragedy—terminal diagnosis, loss of a child, sibling, or parent. For others, the search comes with the loss of a limb, which we are experiencing more frequently in light of the wars in Iraq and Afghanistan.

The question is then posed: how do we find the God of love and mercy when we are up to our ears in alligators? It has been said that pain is God's megaphone. We take God's gift of life for granted. He gets our attention when we are deprived of His graces. Then we develop a serious and meaningful conversation with Him. We ask, "Where are you?" "Do you exist?" "What's going on?" and "Are you going to help me?" Job asked serious and angry questions, "Therefore I will not restrain my mouth; I will complain in the bitterness of my soul. Is it God's pleasure for you to oppress?" (Job 7:11)

The great St. Therese of Avila shared this sentiment when she fell out of her carriage in a wicked rain into the mud. She exclaimed to God, "If this is the way you treat your friends, God, no wonder you have so few of them."

I remember speaking to a delegation of several hundred people in San Juan Capistrano several years ago. I had shared both Job's and St. Therese's frustration when a woman in the audience challenged me, saying, "Isn't this sacrilegious? I find this offensive to God." I responded, "Do you believe that God desires an intimate relationship with us? And does that involve honesty?" I believe intimacy demands it.

I found this interaction with her profound as it brought to the fore a definition of relationship and its superficiality. Relationship, as defined by *Webster's*, is the quality or state of being connected. I pose the question, can we truly be connected without truth or honesty?

I believe firmly that our God desires intimacy, and that involves sharing not just our joy but also our sadness, anger, heartaches, and frustrations. If He is God, doesn't He know it all anyway? Who do we think we are fooling? The Supreme Being who made and knows all things?

I know God is the only one who can initiate healing. He is the unseen *hand* wanting to comfort us (Hebrews 13:2). He delivers us and sends His angels to encamp around us when we engage with Him and honor Him (Psalm 34:8).

Thomas Merton, one of the great twentieth-century contemplatives said, "The saint is not one who accepts suffering because he likes it. He may hate it as much as anyone, but he so loves Christ, whom he does not see, that he will allow his love to be proven by any suffering."

Let then the prayer be God, I seek Your peace and presence. Let Your perfect love fill my heart with spiritual joy. Help me to relax in Your love. Fill me with a faith that takes me through my difficulty because I know, Father, that You have planned every detail of my life. I totally trust in You.

The Way of the Cross Is Not for Sissies

None of us can escape our humanity. No one ever said life is a piece of cake. Many, I have met along the way, believe God is upset, unhappy, and disappointed in us. That's why we suffer. I know God loves us! He made us in His image and likeness to be heirs of His kingdom. He died that we might have life with Him. The Resurrection is our Easter promise.

The search, which is also the way of the cross, *can be* difficult and often challenging. Just read the paper, turn on the television, or look around in your home and community. Sickness, death, suffering, and violence surround us. This realization does not preclude finding peace.

The search means going within. I have often heard it said, "God hid all His secrets within us because He knew it was the last place we would look." How true!

We need to trust the promise of the one born in a manger. He is the only one who rescues. We find Him in silence and within. "Be still and know that I am God" (Psalm 46:10). In Him, we find the love and joy we seek.

Is it easy? Was it easy for the Man-God? You know! He was scourged, mocked, beaten, spat upon, crowned with thorns, and crucified; He thought we were worth it. Did He suffer? Did He ask, if possible, that this cup pass? Jesus, the Man-God, was so in Divine will that He gave His total fiat to God, and you know the rest. His resurrection is the streaming light in our lives that illuminates every moment of the day. He died that we might have life to the fullest in Him. This is the Easter of our lives!

How about the Mother Mary? (Luke 1:26–38). The angel Gabriel said, "Hail, favored one, the Lord is with you. Do not be afraid." Mary said, "Behold I am the handmaiden of the Lord. May it be done to me according to your word." Mary would watch her Son—the perfect Son, perfect love—die mercilessly on the cross for all of us. She knew for a lifetime (Simeon's prophecy, Luke 2:25–35) that He would be taken from her and yet united her will to God's—the ultimate sacrifice, the ultimate act of love.

God orchestrated all this for our redemption. Do we ever ponder the sacrifices made for us to ensure eternal life? Do we ever ponder God, much less life eternal?

While touring the United States for my first book, *Be a Light*, I heard repeatedly, "I go from meeting to meeting all day. I have responsibilities—babies, baths, recitals, soccer, cooking, work, practice, and games. I just don't have time to ponder." I also heard, "I'm so busy and so tired. There just isn't enough time to pray. You say a prayer for me." Sound familiar?

Suggested prayer: God, still my mind and help me to want you. Help me to know you. Open my eyes and heart to a future with you. Give me the patience and courage to persevere and know your peace.

Prayer and Connection

We are all products of our environment or, as some prefer to express it to me, victims of victims. We are programmed at an early age. I was taught to recite certain prayers. Maybe you were too. Much like a parrot, I could and would recite words without thought.

It was in 1981 when I first went to a holy place called Medjugorje, Yugoslavia, on a dare from a then-atheist fellow news reporter. The experience changed my life. Six children (at the time) were receiving visions from the Mother Mary, Queen of Peace. I was astounded to find these children of average appearance and was told by church hierarchy that they were not particularly spiritual before the "phenomena" began. More astounding was the fact that each connected with God in a different manner. One had conversations with God, one would meditate, one would repeatedly recite the rosary, one would read the Bible, etc.

Was there a message in this observation? Could it be that God meets us where we are? We worry about style and form. Maybe Jesus is just looking for sincere hearts. The fact that each child was different from the other and quite ordinary in their likes and dislikes spoke volumes to my heart. Could it be that God is not looking for the extraordinary, but that these children represent all of us—a small microcosm of the world? Could God be calling ordinary people to extraordinary acts? Is He willing to meet each right where He is? I believe this to be true. Is He saying we are enough right where we are with His grace to cope with the seemingly impossible? Is Medjugorje an invitation to seek Him? "Knock and the door shall be opened" (Matthew 7:7).

Little did I know that the Medjugorje experience would, much like a tapestry, unfold and become a major influence in a future life crisis.

I had been traveling the world, places like Italy and Venezuela, lecturing on Medjugorje and its meaning, doing healing services with a Benedictine abbot, praying with and for the sick and dying. This was the greatest privilege and grace of my life. For a long time, I did this with total joy, commitment and the grace of God.

Ann Marie's Spiritual director Abbot Benedict
Mary Mother of The Church Abbey (Virginia)
at National Shrine Washington (on right)

Diagnosis

It was fall of 2012 when my world would change, my peace would be disturbed, and life altered. My own mother was diagnosed with cancer. She had not been to a doctor in forever. She was always healthy, as was my father who volunteered at the local hospital each week and played tennis each Wednesday at the age of eighty-seven.

Life had, to this point, been so beautiful, uncomplicated, and blessed. In an instant and in my own family, everything would change. This was personal!

Mom did not tell me she had cancer. She had not called me or anyone to drive her to the doctor's office that day. Mom was always strong-willed and private, not given to intimate or personal conversation, not even with family.

It was my dad who called me and said he wanted to talk to me. This rarely happened. Mom always handled phone calls and always answered when family would call. My mom was always in control.

It's funny what you remember at a time like this. I remember getting engaged to my husband of forty-eight years and asking Mom for marital advice. She said, "You know what you need to know." That was the end of the conversation. I remembered a massive bug infestation in army housing at Fort Monroe in 1973. Tommy was on active duty at the time. I was totally traumatized by what I saw and came home for a couple days. When I described my emotional state to Mom, she said, "Get over it. There are worse things." She was watching Archie Bunker.

Mom was very private. I think I saw her in her slip twice in my life. She emerged every morning dressed and in full makeup. *Private!*

This information is significant in term of Mom's cancer journey. I asked her why she didn't call me. The response, "No big deal."

I asked, "What specifically did the doctor say? What's the prognosis and type of cancer?"

"Ann, drop it! I don't want to talk about it."

We know, intellectually, that denying something doesn't lessen its seriousness or improve the chances of its disappearance. There is a time for conversation, but I knew she needed to process and digest the news her way. Part of love is respect. I thought, at some point, we would talk and she would cry. Me too. We never had the conversation every daughter or son needs to have. She wouldn't have it. Mom was a closed shop!

We do sickness and/or death on the sick person's terms. We encourage whatever gives them peace. For Mom, it was Nora Roberts' books and good food, comfort food, when she could eat. It was Notre Dame football and VCU basketball.

The third example of life with Mom and another turning point in my life happened in 1971. Tommy and I were stationed at Fort Leonard Wood, Missouri. I was having a challenging pregnancy. I was sent home to deliver for medical reasons. Born on my husband's birthday, our daughter passed away from hyaline membrane disease two days later. After Stacy's burial, the doctor insisted I stay at home in Richmond for a few weeks so my body could recuperate.

Mom came in one morning and said, "Stacy's gone. It's time to move on. We have a wedding in the family. It's not your time now. It's your sister's." This is not about judging Mom. I loved her as you will see. She and all of us do the best we can based on what we are given. We are all victims of victims. We do not all have the same tools in our box.

Journey

Mom's cancer diagnosis was no different. "We're not talking about it. We are moving on." So often in life if we do not acknowledge our lessons, our God allows the next step to get our attention.

Mom's little pink speck above her eyebrow was barely visible in May. She put a Band-Aid on it, and by September 8, my niece's wedding, she had a large white gauze on her forehead in the wedding pictures. All the persistent questions precipitated a September visit to the doctor. On September 20, an all-day surgery was performed on Mom, removing the better part of the top of her head. She gave the appearance of a little Egyptian mummy with her large turban and just her eyes, nose, and mouth exposed. There was a tube in the back of her head for drainage (which she later removed herself).

At eighty-nine years old and in the condition described, after one day, the doctor asked if she was ready to go home. I had spent the night with Mom and found myself responding for her with an emphatic "No, she's not going home today." I wondered how Jesus felt when he threw the money changers out of the temple.

The elderly and sick of *all* ages need—must have—an advocate and one that is not easily impressed or intimidated. I know this from, at least, four experiences with hospitals and well-intentioned doctors. My advice: be not afraid, speak your mind, trust yourself, and be firm when you speak. Nobody knows your loved one better than you do. Pay attention to the medications. Ask the questions about drug interactions. If pain medication isn't cutting it, walk down that hall and respectfully ask for something more. No one should yell in pain with so many new medical advances. Always ask. Don't be shy!

Our parents grew up in an era of doctor worship. We pay these wonderful people for an educated guess. As a loved one, if you strongly feel something is wrong, it probably is.

I have been in intensive care too many times to recall due to a rare health problem. I've been in a life-threatening situation repeatedly when doctors argue with a medical letter from Duke requesting a glucose IV prep as I have a toxic allergy to sodium (my heart stopped at the age of fifty). My husband has been my advocate forever and I am his.

Hancock's experience at Duke has affirmed her faith.

YOU CAN'T DRIVE YOUR CAR TO YOUR OWN FUNERAL

Ann Marie Hancock with Dr. Frank Neelon, who put her on the Rice Diet and on the road to health.

Medicine and miracles

Dad, however, was very dependent on Mom. She paid the bills, did the laundry, and fixed his meals. Dad hated hospitals. When I delivered each of my four children, Dad would peek in and congratulate, and he was gone, often telling me how he felt about blood and hospitals. I'd had four C-sections, the old way. The doctor asked Dad if he wanted to see how nicely I was healing and displayed the scar. Dad said, "Looks like a big zipper" and almost passed out. Once again, he was gone. I never questioned why my dad couldn't stay. It was simple for me. He just couldn't.

As I have aged, I now wonder if it had something to do with his mom dying when he was a little boy. I've also wondered if it had to do with being placed in an orphanage as a young boy and then lying about his age to join the Marine Raiders at fifteen years old and then being at Guadalcanal, one of the bloodiest battles of WWII. You see, it's so easy to judge when we don't have all the facts and background at our disposal. I never doubted that my dad loved me as best he could.

Dad called me over to Krim Point (home) to tell me Mom had cancer. He broke down and cried. This was a new territory for me. My dad was a tough guy, sometimes scary, and he was broken. I wanted to fix him, but only God could do that. He wouldn't let you hold him. The man who never had a childhood cried. I wondered how many times he had cried in his life. I knew he cried when our daughter died. I knew he walked out of the funeral home and left my young husband because he couldn't handle it. It's funny; I never judged him, just wondered about his life and his pain and what I was never told. I said a prayer for him.

My dad would remain broken and seemed very relieved that I spent that night in the hospital with Mom. He would never be the same.

Mom, on the other hand, returned home from her first surgery and refused to take pain medication and, at eighty-nine years old, feared pain pill addiction. It would be a couple of days before she would remove the turban and drainage tube and view the new mama in the mirror.

At the same time I was going back and forth from my house to hers with flowers and meals daily. Mom never mentioned the unveiling, and I intuitively knew not to address it.

The next month found Mom feisty, refusing to say the word *cancer* and back at her favorite stop and shop, Walmart (three miles from her home).

In late October and without family knowledge, she drove herself to the oncologist for a checkup. A biopsy was ordered, and on November 5, Mom reported to Dad that the cancer had moved to the lymph system and more surgery was needed. The fabulous Dr. Alan Burke would perform the delicate facial surgery on the parotid gland. My dad would not live to see the second surgery.

Unexpected Event

Dad had, in the last two months, developed high blood pressure and even experienced chest pains at Mass one Sunday and dismissed them. Mom's rediagnosis of cancer and the November election took a terrible toll on him. His candidate lost the presidential election.

On November 8, sometime during the night, my dad got up to go to the bathroom, had a heart attack, and died. I remember it like yesterday. The call came at 5:30 a.m. I thought Mom was in trouble, but my dad had passed. I was shocked. I felt like I was moving through some misty fog. Our daughter, Faith, came to pick me up. I don't remember dressing. Tommy was out of town for the week. I knew I had to be a big girl for my mom, my children, and my grandchildren.

We were told he went quickly. I had a feeling he would go first because he kept saying "What am I gonna do?" He just couldn't get himself together. During Mom's first surgery, he was a wreck. He had to go outside the hospital more than once and couldn't stop crying. I could feel his fear. We know that fear paralyzes. We were not able to console him.

It was after 6:00 a.m. on November 8 when they came for Dad. He was lying on his side on his bedroom floor. I still remember the exit with the American flag draped over him. Time seemed to stand still. No time to grieve. The funeral parlor wanted to see us in one hour and a half with a written obituary. I still remember putting it together on the drive there.

I would suggest to you to exercise great caution when choosing someone for funeral arrangements. While it sounds easy, it is better for everyone to have a self-chosen option in which you and the family will later be comfortable. Do your homework. For this is a time of frayed nerves, fragility, and great fatigue. Emotions are unpredictable.

Maybe this has something to do with forgetting that life is a short journey leading to eternal love and light, our real destination, our purpose for being here. Earth is not our home but a stopping place to be used wisely and lovingly on our journey back to God.

It was interesting to observe Mom. What still stands out in my mind is the compassionate priest asking her at the cemetery if he could help her in any way. She said, "Nope, I'm going home to watch Notre Dame football."

I wondered what she was thinking or feeling or if she would let herself feel. Was she stoic for us? Was she still in shock? I don't know. I will never know, but this I knew: she had to think about her cancer journey without her spouse of sixty-seven years and her future. Wow!

Planning for the Inevitable

Someone once quipped that 99.9 percent of us will die at some point in our lives. My parents were in their mid-eighties when they finally faced the probability that they were not going to be in the one-tenth of a percent who were going to attain immortality. It was then that they took a number of steps, which, in the end, would be of great benefit to their children as they dealt with post-death obligations.

They met with an attorney, updated their wills, affirmed their visions for the distribution of their assets, discussed financial planning options such as trusts, transfer on death (TOD) provisions for investment accounts, and others designed to streamline their estate-settling process and reduce the financial/emotional impact of death from probate, legal, and accounting fees and taxes. They selected an executor and alternate whom they trusted to carry out their directives as expressed in their wills and obtained their consents to serve. In order to be prepared should there be a period before death in which they may not be able to attend to routine business affairs, they had general power of attorneys prepared naming their executor as the attorney-in-fact. In our case, this was very helpful. During the last few weeks of Mom's life, there were routine bills of hers, utilities and the like, for which payments were due and a few tasks that Mom wanted accomplished, which the attorney-in-fact was authorized to handle for her.

They met with their executor and discussed their intentions in detail. They provided him with a copy of their wills and a list of assets, including accounts numbers, passwords, balances, and the location of key documents such as deeds, car titles, insurance policies, investment statements, contracts, etc.

They selected and purchased a cemetery section and monuments. I mentioned writing my dad's obituary while driving to the funeral parlor the day of his unexpected passing. Mom learned from that experience and later wrote her own obituary, complete with picture that she selected, and put it in a file for her executor.

Mom and Dad prepared as best they could for a smooth transition. My sisters and I were very grateful. Their example should be a lesson for all of us. The siblings were however trying to focus on the present and mom's needs.

Refocusing

I cried privately quiet tears for what was left unsaid, for what could have been and never was. I had to refocus on Mom and the next surgery, the longest one. This one was grueling and took place in December before Christmas. I tried daily to open doors for Mom to say anything she wanted to other than "Whaddya bring me for lunch or dinner?" The silence was sometimes deafening! There was little conversation and sometimes outright *anger*.

The family was all there for this surgery, and it was an all-day affair. We were not permitted to see her in recovery until after midnight. She was a pitiful sight. There were no dry eyes. To see her and ponder all she had been through in three months was overwhelming. Faith and Mike have two children, and Faith teaches school. She magically appeared at eight in the evening at the hospital with a vase of flowers, saying, "My grandma is going to wake up with flowers."

Flowers are so symbolic. We celebrate with them—birthdays, weddings, anniversaries—and we grieve with them. Which would it be?

We went home after 1:00 a.m. only to scurry back to Hanover county in the morning to find her walking down the hall with assistance. She was very unhappy with her room. I was very grateful to find her alive. After two nights, Mom said, "I'm out of here. I can't sleep." The noise from the adjacent rooms disturbed her greatly. The noise, not the operation.

I was so fatigued that I didn't wait for an elevator but chose the stairs and promptly fell. My hip would never be the same. I didn't want Mom to know; she had enough on her plate, so I excused myself and announced I'd be back later. The next time I saw Mom, I had a cane. My hip got worse, so I saw a surgeon and discovered the hip was bone on bone. Surgery was scheduled but later postponed because of a nasty spider bite that landed me in the hospital for two weeks and initially interrupted my breathing.

The hip pain went from bad to worse and put me in a wheelchair, which I alternated with a rollator. My surgery was moved to November.

In the meantime, Tommy and I took Mom to consults, CAT scans, MRIs, heart surgeons, cancer surgeons, back surgeons, her GP, dentist, etc.

In January, a month after her second operation, Tommy and I took her back to Dr. Burke. He scheduled a gold eyelid insert. It was supposed to be a relatively easy and short surgery. I arrived at St. Mary's in Richmond on a cold morning at six. I did not see Mom again until four thirty that afternoon in recovery. Tommy was out of town. Our daughter, Faith, came with the children and brought me lunch and stayed in the waiting room. Later that evening, she picked up prescriptions and meds while driving around with her two small children, Maddie and Jack.

God does send those angels to encamp when we need them. Faith's name is no accident. She is the little girl we weren't supposed to have, but remember God can do anything.

Radiation

Later that week, Mom started radiation. I asked her if she wanted to postpone it. Her comment, "Let's get on with it." I spent weeks with Mama in her daily radiation in the mornings. I would leave her each day around 4:30, and we'd eat lunch if she felt like it. If not, I'd get her settled in her bed at home and make sure she had her pills, books, food, drink, and straws. It was during radiation that her appetite waxed and waned. Some days she wanted a bloody Mary and wanted to eat out, other days a bowl of bland chicken broth with a straw.

I would take my cues from Mama. I learned her moods from quiet to totally distracted with meaningless chatter. I learned to go with the flow and not take offense to things she'd say. I knew Mom was scared to death. She felt comfortable striking out at me because she knew I'd take it and come back for more, and I did day after day. When God is with you, no one can stand against you.

Mom refused to move in with us, citing her independent spirit. "I like my house, my TV, my Andy Griffith and Archie Bunker. I like doing what I want when I want."

I get it. When you have called the shots for seventy years, you have a life pattern and routine. You don't want babysitters. You want your life the way it *was*! So as long as you can safely honor this, you do! You respect her choices; you come from love and patience, and love allows.

You intuitively know when you need to assert yourself for her safety. Trust me, you know.

I watched Mama every day through the glass at Johnston-Willis Hospital until she disappeared where I couldn't go—radiation. Mama is short and has a quick step. She'd come flying out of there and say let's get a hot chocolate.

It was February 5 when Mom cried. "Uncle . . . Ann," she said, without looking at me, "I'm done. Don't be mad at me." I said, "Mama, it's your choice, your journey. I can share in it, but you are in charge. You do what you need to do for you." There's something to be said for the quality of life. She was done for then. But she would face radiation again a year later.

The PRRFEC Camry

Mom was approaching ninety-one and concerned only about her driving privileges and the reissuance of her license. License plates that read PRRFEC were on her Toyota Camry. We told Mom we would take her anywhere she wanted to go any time. The family matriarch replied, "I am an independent woman and need my wheels. I have things to do." PRRFEC!

I was remembering a trip for lunch with our son, an adventure that would take us to Richmond's west end. Mom directed and said she'd pick *me* up. Arguing was fruitless. She proceeded to run two red lights. After the second episode, I said, "Mom, I think you went through that light." She said, "Don't worry about it. Your dad did it all the time." Mom was strong, tough, and insistent on her independence. I learned to pick my battles. I tried to discourage her from driving. Should I have taken the car? Maybe. She said, "Ann, you drive like Moses." I said, "When did you see Moses drive?" She said, "You're not funny."

Mom was a determined, strong woman! Heaven help anyone who challenged her.

The Routine

I could tell that, *initially*, she seemed embarrassed that I brought meals each day. Her embarrassment was channeled as anger. "I don't want it. Stop bringing food. There's too much et cetera et cetera day after day, the same."

Then one day, she said, "Whatcha got? Come in and sit with me." Before I left, she thanked me and expressed concern that I was wearing myself out. Independent folks are used to doing, *not* being served. It translates "dependence," and they hate that.

Sickness involves humility and accepting help from those who love you. Mom really struggled with this.

So many things come to mind. At or near the top of the list is the question of filters. Often, the sick and elderly lose their filters. I recall, each week, when Mom felt like it, we'd go to lunch with one of my friends. I'm blessed to have fabulous and compassionate friends. One showed Mom a picture of her daughter's new beau. Mom commented, "Wow, he's fat." I wanted to go under the table until I remembered that Mom is not me. I am not Mom. Why was I owning the embarrassment while Mom took a big bite out of her chicken salad?

Another incident that comes to mind immediately is the frequent visit to the heart doctor. His office was on a top floor at the end of a hall at St. Francis Hospital. Mom insisted I drop her off at the front door of the hospital. The doctor's office was at the back entrance and upstairs. I didn't argue. Mom was tired and frightened. She was losing weight quickly, nauseous, and in pain. I parked the car and took the back elevator up. Mom had not arrived upstairs. I got a queasy feeling in my stomach as she stepped off the elevator and flew by me to ask the nurse, "Why the hell is the heart doctor on a top floor and way down at the end of the hall!" After telling anyone who would listen they needed their heads examined, we went to our little exam room where Mom's blood pressure was off the charts. She argued that it was fine when she took it at home. We could not leave until the pressure reached a normal range.

Upon leaving, it was 1:00 p.m., and I asked Mom if she wanted to go to her favorite sandwich shop. Angrily she said, "No, take me home." She popped out of the car with her cane and turban, told me she'd see me tomorrow, and went inside the house.

I knew that she was tired, scared, and even lonely with Dad gone. She was very angry—angry that she didn't see the dermatologist sooner, angry at aggressive squamous cell cancer, angry with herself. She needed some privacy to process or even to cry. I wanted to hold her, but I knew this was not the time. I peacefully pulled away only to return the next day, a new day.

I remember Forest Gump saying "Life is like a box of chocolates. You never know what you're going to get." Just be ready.

Wounded Healer

I have prayed with thousands of people all over the world. Each person is different. The one commonality is that I was invited to pray. These people were happy to see me. Many were so kind and grateful. It has been the greatest privilege of my life to visit and pray with the sick. They are so real, there is no pretense. They are so humble. What a blessing.

Ann Marie and Mother Teresa's order at the National Shrine, Washington

YOU CAN'T DRIVE YOUR CAR TO YOUR OWN FUNERAL

Abbot Benedict McDermott – Spiritual Director also Ann Marie with St. Padre Pio's official photographer, Bill Carrigan, holding objects belonging to Padre Pio (now sainted)

Divine Mercy portrait and Sister Gratia from Saint Faustina's Order in Poland

Mom was different. She wasn't always happy to see me. She was often angry with me, critical of my driving and even of my food choices.

It's as if God said, "OK, Ann Marie, what now? How are you gonna handle this?" I know He needed me to step back, reassess, and remember He is in control. I learned not to take the anger and criticism personally. I know Mom loved me. When we are sick, really sick, love manifests in many ways. We have to dig deeply, go within, keep our composure, and remember who we truly are—God's children.

It isn't easy. We are human, and we all have good days and really challenging days. My hip surgery was several months away, and I was vulnerable. There was lots of self-talk and getting back on the horse.

I would always remember the night in the hospital after the first surgery. Mom would not sleep. It was just the two of us, and there were periodic vital sign checks. She let me hold her hand all night. About 3:00 a.m., she was uncomfortable. As I went to seek a nurse, she turned to me and said, "Ann, you are so gentle with me." There were tears in her eyes. I will never forget that moment. I carry it even now in my heart as I remember a frightened little girl speaking softly and kindly and even gratefully.

When everything goes south, as it did many times, I remember that silent night and Mom. It was a few days later at home when I called Mom. She didn't answer. I didn't want to panic her. I waited fifteen minutes and called again, and she still didn't answer. I got in my car with a trench coat over my pajamas. She didn't answer the door. I was reluctant to use my key. I always knocked out of respect for her privacy. Not this time. I went in to find her washing herself on the bed. She was OK this time, but there would be another time when I found her crying, dehydrated, nauseous, and in pain. I called the oncologist and brought the phone to her. She hung up on him. I called my sister. She hung up on her. This is the most desperate and out of control I ever saw her.

I spoke softly, "Mom, we need help. We can't stay at the house today. We must go to the hospital." I called the tender-hearted nurse I liked on her private phone. Mom refused to talk to her. I became firm. "We're going to the hospital. I'm calling an ambulance, Mom."

Never has she talked so directly to me. There was both pity and rage in those hazel eyes. Something told me if I stayed, calmed her, and fed her water with a straw, she might be more agreeable. I stayed the night. She did not go to the hospital.

    A week later, she called me early in the morning. She was going to Walmart to shop. She was emphatic about going alone. I'd give her two hours and show up with lunch. I observed something strange and made a mental note. Mom didn't need anything. She would buy something and return it a few days later. It was obvious that she had issued an ultimatum to herself. "I will be independent. I will drive my own car. I must do things for myself or else I will lose the confidence and ability to do so. And so she would buy and return. She would insist that she was only out for a minute.

Complications

Her winter trip to intensive care at St. Francis found her with cellulitis. Her legs were oozing fluid and some blood. They were the size of watermelons. The physician asked my sister and me what she'd been doing. We directed questions to Mom about her outings. She denied being out very long.

I was also remembering that she would not show you her head, which was always covered, nor would she tell you her weight.

There came a time I needed to know. Mom appeared to be wearing somebody else's clothes. They were way too big. She'd gone from 178 to below 120 pounds. Only once in a while would she say, "I used to have a full bosom," still refusing to use the word *cancer*.

In May of 2014, she complained regularly about her back hurting. Once again, she refused to see an orthopedist for a couple of months. She said she needed to exercise more. The pain worsened. Finally and on her own, she randomly selected an orthopedic surgeon from the phone book. Incompatibility lead to more frustration for her, I suggested an alternative physician. The appointment was made by her. I picked Mom up. I noticed she was really struggling. We arrived. She had the wrong day. I pushed for her to be seen, but the response was no. We rescheduled. At that time, the doctor ordered a CAT scan. We would return again to find that Mom had a mass in her lung and on her spine. She also had a fracture in her spine.

Now we needed the oncologist. We needed help quickly.

Mom *never* addressed her lung or the mass. Mom would insist that the fracture in her spine could be fixed, and she had seen the guy who would fix it in a television commercial. Dealing with Mama would be touch and go. She became angrier and angrier. And I? I was remembering the story of Jesus in the storm sleeping when the disciple woke Him and said, "Teacher, don't you care if we drown?" (Mark 4:38). Surely, we have all asked at different times in our lives, "Why me?" No one escapes the treachery of sickness and pain. Anyone present at these times can be a target and temporarily claim victim status. But this serves no one. Love requires patience and true confidence, which is faith.

I did feel, at times, I was drowning; I know Mom was sinking. The patient needs to vent, and if you have taken up the select cross of being the target, you need to know that, in a strange way, it is a backhanded compliment that Mom is comfortable enough to choose you. She knows you won't walk away. She eventually acknowledges that you are in it for the long haul. It is difficult. Maybe the most difficult task is to love the unlovable. We are all unlovable at times. Thank God everyone doesn't give up on us. It would be easy to do.

Mothers and daughters have a special bond. We are connected by more than the umbilical cord and for a lifetime. Many spend their lives trying to prove themselves to their parents. We become overachievers; we dance to their song and live according to their rules because we are all looking for love, looking for acceptance.

Right to left
Mom, daughter Cori, Ann Marie and daughter Faith
Mother's Day 2008

But there is a point in time that many also realize that they perform for a congregation of one—God. He alone is the one to please, the one who rescues.

A loving God wants us to love our neighbor (Mom) as self. Love begins with self. Part of this lesson is boundaries. Part of love is respect; it goes two ways.

I remember heading north on Charter Colony with Mom. She had another doctor's appointment. I picked her up at nine in the morning. She was quiet until she belted out, "You moron, where the hell are you going?"

I responded, "To the doctor's—"

She said, "Are you a moron? What have you been drinking?" I had to smile. Mom's heritage is Irish and her family name is Moran. In Ireland, the proper pronunciation of Moran is "more-on," so I guess I am a moron; we are family of morons.

I responded, "No and coffee. What's the problem?"

She said, "*You.*"

I knew this wasn't going to be one of our better mornings, and I definitely felt the joy sucked right out of me. It was like being five years old again when you were sent to your room for doing a little artwork on the dining room walls. Yes, the same nauseating feeling was coming back to this sixty-plus-year-old daughter. Yup! She can still get to me. But what's different? Me. I knew I was doing the best that I could, and I was calm, even finding a little humor in the situation.

While driving, I calmly said, "Mama, tell me the problem."

She said, "You're a moron and going the wrong way."

I said, "Are we not going to see Dr. Glenn?"

She said, "No, Dr. Kapadia."

I said, "Mama, I will turn around at the corner."

She said, "You are wasting your husband's gas, and you always go around your elbow to get to your thumb!"

I said, "Yup."

It's a funny thing. I always thought Tommy's gas was my gas since we've been married for forty-eight years. There is no yours or mine in our marriage, except for clothing.

Unwanted Messages

Everything is in our computers, and it begins in the womb. The little or big messages crop up during our lives to test us and see how we are progressing. We either fold or smile and remember who we are—children of God, all of us.

You know you are doing well if you don't wreck the car and don't own every message given to you. I learned this during my years at NBC as on-air talent when you leave the studio after shows.

I had an Afro in the late '70s, and the messages were like the following: "Did Ann Marie stick her finger in a light switch?" Other messages were worse. You learn to tune in and tune out. When I was pregnant, TV messages were "Tell Ann Marie to stay out of the donuts. She's starting to look like the Pillsbury Doughboy."

We can cry or consider the source. Some messages resonate, but many do not. Don't own them.

Mom and I would have many challenging days, and I just assumed the Lord would still work with me on the virtue of patience. Patience is not my long suit.

As Mom felt worse, I remember a day in Dr. Glenn's office. It was packed! Mom walked in with a cane that held a saber in it. Dad had given it to her for Valentine's Day. But this day, I was afraid she'd use it on office personnel. We had been waiting thirty minutes when Mom took the cane to the reception desk and said, "Hey, what's going on? We were here first. This is not right." I couldn't look and had a vision of us in the *Times-Dispatch*: "Mother and Daughter Slay Nurses for Time Delay in Office." They were kind at first, saying they had a full schedule at which time Mom said, "I don't care. Get us in there."

Mom was to revisit the reception desk and did not receive a warm welcome. She would excoriate many doctors and nurses.

This is not about judgment. This is about fear. Fear manifests in many ways. Fear, manifests as anger, can be rage, anxiety, hatred, and jealousy. Most or all, negative emotion comes from fear—fear of dying, fear of living, fear of not being enough, fear of not being loved.

In my many years of participating in healing services all over the world, the one statement I heard over and over again is "How can God love me? God won't heal me. I'm nobody. I'm not good enough." This is powerful stuff. Fear keeps us from our own personal truth. "We are loved."

Why don't people remember that God created us all in His image and likeness to be heirs of His kingdom? That's a lot of love. Why would perfect God choose to love one group and create another group for failure? Why bother? Does a mother love one child more than another? Each child is a gift. And God's love is infinite!

Let the prayer be: Sweet Jesus, help my unbelief. Give me the true confidence, the faith to know I am loved beyond my comprehension. Help me to remember that I am your child and strive to be worthy of the privilege.

Managing Mom

Mom started having worse days. I hired a nurse (home health). Mom, again, refused to come and live with Tom and me, citing her independence. Her wish was to remain in her home and out of nursing care. But in truth, it was becoming more challenging. When Mom didn't answer her phone in the morning, I would call and call again, put a trench coat over my nightgown, and drive to her home fifteen minutes away by the interstate. Sometimes, she didn't feel like answering. Other times she would say she was busy. I concluded I needed assistance and interviewed a nurse. Angela was lovely with a cherubic face. I felt she would have a calming effect on Mom. She came three times, and Mom fired her. Mom said, "It's a waste of time. I don't want her, and I won't pay for her."

Time marched on, and there was one day I found Mom in dire straits and crying. It seemed strange to see her cry. She was so tough. She said, "I'm so sick and sick of being sick."

"What can I do, Mom? What would you like me to do? How can I help?"

She said, "Go home to your own family."

I rehired the nurse, and Mom fired her again.

Sometimes, Mom would come to the farm (my home) for a two-day stay. Never more. She always had to get home. We have a large brindle-colored English mastiff. Mom and Barli were like oil and water. Mom called our dog a bipolar mess. This did not make for an endearing relationship with our 168-pound dog. Mom would sit in a big soft chair, look down at Barli, and yell, "You are bipolar." Barli would get up and go under the dining room table. Mom would say, "I'm going to touch that dog before I die." She never did. She never dared.

The year before Mom passed, the Hancocks had a large Christmas party. We thought the joy and laughter might be balm for Mom's soul. We invited my husband's hospital law associates, hospital administrators, and other friends. Mom walked in to Christmas music and sounds of "Silver Bells," approached a hospital CEO, and said, "I have a bone to pick with you." Then she listed her complaints about the hospital. I decided I'd have a lemon drop (fun martini). It didn't help.

YOU CAN'T DRIVE YOUR CAR TO YOUR OWN FUNERAL

The Hancock Family (L to R): Front Row: Kendall, Jack, Maddie;
Second Row: Dan, Cori, Ann Marie, Faith, Mike;
Third Row: Chase, Tom, Chip, Ann.

I decided, long ago, Mom is Mom, and I loved her no matter what. I'm me, and she is Mom. Her comments are her own.

"Lord, help us to love everyone right where they are. Help me to remember my own boo-boos when I'm quick to judge. Lord, make me a channel of your love. Help me to speak as you would, to hear as you hear, to act as you would. In God's name, I humbly request your help."

In her writings, Elizabeth Kubler Ross references stages of grieving as denial, anger, bargaining, depression, and acceptance. These stages apply, as she points out, to big life losses, permanent losses (death), and small losses, for instance the loss of an opportunity or job, scholarship, etc.

There is *no* specific order to grieving. Some (as Mom) just stay angry right to the end. I remember taking Mom for the last time to her oncologist. The appointment was less than five minutes. I tried to hold her hand. She jerked it away, saying, "Stop, I'm fine." Profound. "I'm fine." She said, "I'm done, I won't be back." She got her cane with the saber, started out of the room, turned, and said, "Unless I have more pain." She never returned.

The Hancocks were heading out the door to Mass one Sunday. The phone rang (I thought) as we walked out the door late. On the way to Mass, our daughter, Faith, called me and said, "Leenie has fallen in her garage, and we have taken her to the hospital." We turned around and headed for St. Francis. Mom had entered with our daughter and her family through the emergency room, her face covered with blood, I could hardly recognize her. She looked to be a little child—so fragile, so little, almost unrecognizable. I felt absolutely sick. The best I could say was "Hey, Mom, how are you doing?" She said, "I want out of here." Tumors in her lung, fractures in her spine, cellulitis, heart attack, and now this. I thought my heart would break. They stitched her head and let her go home (a head that had already suffered the blows of a scalpel and cancer).

She did not want to talk about this or how it happened. She insisted we not make a big deal of it. It was our daughter, Faith, who left the hospital when Tom and I arrived and solved the mystery. She was to go to Mom's house and clean. The family determined that Mom had tried to drive. There was blood everywhere—down the side of her car and a path on the floor of the garage where Mom crawled into her home, across the living room, and handprints to her chair where she reached the phone. She had called Tom and me (maybe the call we thought we heard going out the door), couldn't reach us, and got Faith. Faith spent a long time at her house cleaning the crime scene on her hands and knees so Mom would not have to come home to it. Faith, like Sherlock Holmes, had an educated conjecture as to what happened and could actually track it across the floor of Mom's home and into the garage.

Mom had life alert and *never* used it. She did not want commotion in the neighborhood, didn't want the neighbors upset. She would always insist upon going via family.

The day she had her heart attack, she called my sister at work to come and get her. My sister, concerned for the time element, said, "Call 911 and get an ambulance." The response was "Come and get me."

Mom was very concerned about the neighbors, thinking she was too old and ill to be alone. The question arises. How many falls had she taken? She slipped at the mailbox one day and accused me of overreacting, saying, "I just sort of sat down. Don't be melodramatic." That comment always stings because I had been in television for years and excelled in performing.

Mom was a master. As Mama, she knew everyone's sensitivities or hot spots. I was the child who wore her heart on her sleeve. This was still in my computer, and ego was doing a number on me. In times like this, I needed to remember that Mom was scared, lonely, and in pain. She couldn't verbalize her pain, and so it came out as a rough directive back off.

I was learning a great deal from Mama; moreover, I was keenly aware of all the lessons I had yet to learn about me, life, and people. These days with Mom were humbling. I would ask God each day for the love and courage to return.

Sweet Jesus, thank you for trying to further enhance virtues of patience and compassion in me. You are the foundation of all love and knowledge. You and you alone know Mom's body, mind, and soul. Help me to act as you would and to see your child in her, not to speak unless my words are uplifting and helpful and loving.

ANN MARIE HANCOCK

Singer, Mickey Gilley of Stand By Me fame
being interviewed by Ann Marie

Jane Pauley, NBC

YOU CAN'T DRIVE YOUR CAR TO YOUR OWN FUNERAL

Hollywood publicity shots: Rod Taylor, Ann Marie, and the 'Oregon Trail' co-stars.

Independence

Mom was sneaking out in her car—a little nick here, a little nick there, or unidentified paint here and there. Nobody talked about it. To ask was the curse of death. But soon, Mom would need to renew her driver's license; we would all discourage this by saying, "We'll take you anywhere you want to go." Once again, Mom reinstated her strong independent spirit. "I can drive myself."

Whispering on an early Tuesday morning, Mom's voice crossed the Verizon wires, "I did it. I got it."

"Got what, Mom?"

"My driver's license. I passed. I didn't have to drive. Just read two lines of the eye chart."

I said, "Great, Mom. Are you going home?"

"Nope, I'm going to Walmart."

I would ask Mom daily, "How's your pain?" Her response was always the same seven on a scale of one to ten. She always said seven, followed by "I'm a little stiff." Mom never took the prescribed oxycodone; she only took half. We had several discussions about her pain level and the fact that, in this day and age, there were many things to alleviate suffering.

Even at ninety-one years old, Mom would say, "Ann, I'm not going to be an addict. People get dependent on this stuff."

My beloved Lord, help me to accept and not argue or question Mom's judgment. Help me to know that she needs to do what she needs to do and to remember it's not my journey. It's Mama's. We will all be there one day, realizing we can neither escape death or suffering. What will my behavior be? Will I be responsive to my children usurping my choices and independence? It must be very difficult to be in control for a lifetime and then have your children step in, total role reversal, and tell *you* what to do. I can't imagine, but it gives me a sense of what Mom's feeling and what's coming for all of us.

Personalities are complicated and a composite of everything the senses have taken in for a lifetime. Many questions come into play. It is so easy to judge without thinking. So many questions need to be asked. What is her or his life like? What about the thousands of private moments we know nothing about? What was the marriage like? The childhood? Did he or she have affectionate parents? Supportive and loving? The realm of the unknown and part of all of us. None of us can give what has not been in our experience. We simply can't relate. The dynamic is interesting. Ego comes into play and says, "I'm threatened, I must defend myself." Often in life, I have witnessed counterattack. Often the offensive party is just threatened and crying for help. Sometimes, silence is truly golden because we cannot take our words back. Once they are out in the ethers, they are not forgotten, finding a place in someone's mind and heart forever. I am working very hard on thinking before I speak and holding back and questioning why I interpret comments personally as if they belong to me. I am convinced it is only ego responding with help from alter ego. My heart knows I am loved, but the mind complicates things. This would appear to make life a remembering and a forgetting of who we really are.

We are not living in a loving world. We are a people divided by culture, religion, ethnicity. We have children killing children, children killing parents and vice versa. We have Christian haters (clinging to their guns and religion) and Jewish haters. We are a world that strayed from its heart.

There is no respect for the elderly for their years of experience and wisdom. We are living in a youth-centered and sex-focused world, and we've lost our way. We can't remember what love is. We have become numb or anesthetized. There is so much sadness, violence, hatred, and crime that we do not think or feel anymore; nothing seems to surprise us.

I can't imagine what Mama felt about today's world. She grew up in a small town of a couple hundred people. Everyone walked everywhere. Everyone knew everyone. Everyone went to church. Doors were never locked. A bell rang at noon, and everyone came home for lunch.

People knew one another and responded to one another's needs. Life was simpler. As Mom said, "We talked to one another."

The world today is fast-paced with Twitter, e-mail, iPods, iPads, etc. We send a short text, and often the human element is eliminated. Children live on computers. Mom grew up with "go outside and play." I grew up the same way—chasing butterflies in a cow pasture, capturing pollywogs in the swamp, playing fort with the boys and using my imagination, creating a circus in the garage with stuffed animals, selling tickets for a nickel, dressing up in Mom's old gowns, and playing ballroom or wedding.

Mom has watched a mass transition from the simple life to the electronic revolution. How has this affected her world view?

I can share this. I called Mama at my regular time in the early morning. One morning, she didn't answer. I repeated the process and put my coat on over my night clothes and headed to Krim Point. I knocked, and Mom opened the door. She was in tears.

"Neither my house phone or cell will work. Ann, they're both dead."

I asked, "Why didn't you go next door and call from your neighbor's house? Mom, I was worried."

She said, "It's not their business."

I spent the entire day getting Mom's house phone fixed. We all know the process: push 1, push 2, push 3, push 4, then the recording! Mom was totally frustrated. She was tired, in pain, ninety-one years old, and challenged by all technology.

I told her we would replace her cell phone. She wanted to go to Walmart right away. She had purchased her cell phone there. We were told it couldn't be repaired. The sales clerk told her it was old, inexpensive, and useless. You can imagine her reaction.

We purchased a new one and returned home.

The new one was simple. It had a beach scene for the cover. I told her that when she saw the ocean she could dial, and there was one button to terminate her call. She couldn't grasp this, became angry, and said we might do better with something else.

I personally am not an appreciator of technology. I plead ignorance, but today, I was very aware of how threatening this was to Mom. I told her that if the house phone went out again, go next door to Eleanor's and call me. Her response, "I don't want to worry the neighbors with my problems. It's my business, not theirs."

Our parents grew up with an enormous sense of privacy. Family business was family business and not to be shared. There is a time, however, that we all need help, and there is always help available. So what keeps us from seeking it when in dire straits?

Soul Storm Goes South

I was pondering the Valentine's Day after dad died. My thoughts went to Mom, and I had a brainstorm, maybe a soul storm. Tom and I always went to the beach for Valentine's Day. We had our special haunts that we enjoyed visiting. We would take Mama. This would be her first trip out since her three surgeries. She surely needed a lift. We would visit *her* favorite haunts and dine at her favorite places. We would go at her rate of speed and be totally conscious of her pain and fatigue. We would take all cues from her. We had Valentine surprises, gifts, and cards. Tommy would give her a diamond bracelet. She loved the Virginia Diner. She loved ham. The diner accommodated her with chicken and ham biscuits. She loved peanuts and bought two cans. She appeared happy, and Tom and I were thrilled to see her smile. The jaunt to the beach is about two hours from Richmond. We arrived at the ocean front hotel midafternoon. Mom walked into her oceanfront room, and we had balloons and small gift-wrapped surprises for her. She loved it. We left her to take a nap before dinner. She tapped on our adjoining room, all dressed and excited about dinner downstairs in the hotel. Tommy gave her the bracelet at dinner. She loved it and called him Saint Thomas. Dinner was divine, and then we went back upstairs and tucked her in. We didn't wake her in the morning; we waited for her knock. She wanted eggs Benedict. This was great because her appetite waxed and waned.

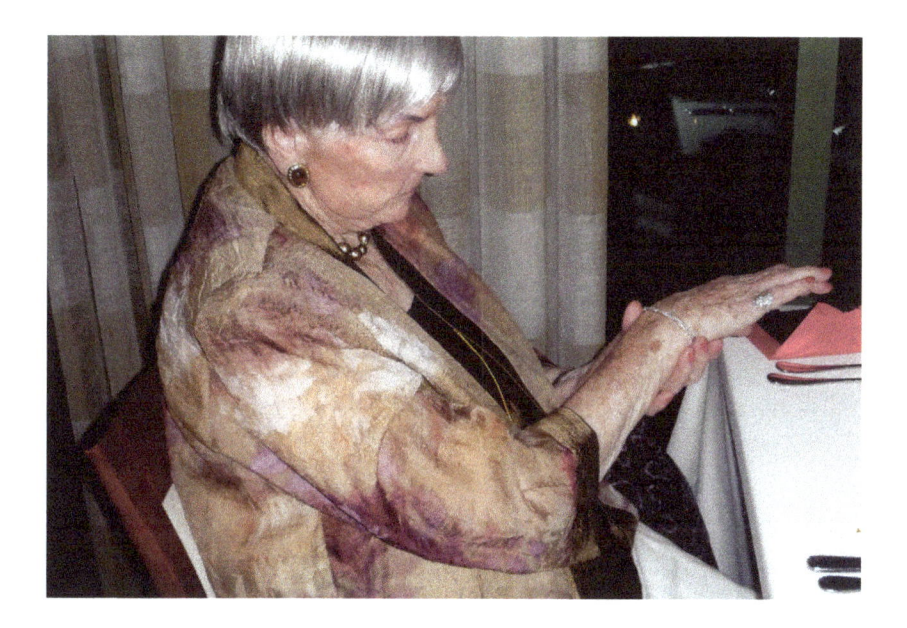

Mom wanted to shop later in the day. There was a bridgeway in the hotel going over the street to shops below. With her trusty cane, we started our walk through the hotel. It was too much for her; we returned for naps.

Dinner was her favorite—fried shrimp at Lynnhaven Fishhouse. We sat by the water. Mom seemed to love it, and she, once again, wore her fancy dress.

We were all happy, and it seemed to be the perfect Valentine's weekend until we returned to the hotel.

A lovely woman greeted us in the lobby. She was from Pennsylvania, just like Mom, and she was a guide for the hotel. She'd worked there for many years and was steeped in the history of the beach and the hotel. She asked if we'd like to go to the upper floor and see some of the art and photographs. Tom and I deferred to Mom who said, "Sure." The tour was amazing, and the woman was a walking encyclopedia, even including a story about Walt Disney.

She was mid-sentence when Mom interrupted her to ask about something she'd just explained. She looked at Mom, who was about the same age, give or take a few years, and said, "You're a cute little thing, but you need to listen and not talk so much." I could feel the floor swallow me up. I couldn't even look at Mom. The guide, unaffected by her own comment, just smiled and continued speaking. I wanted to throw up on my shoes. I knew, at that moment, that the weekend was over, not just the tour.

All the gifts, surprises, and meals could not make up for the guide's words. I knew it. Mom said nothing, but breakfast the next and last morning would be the big reveal. She began, "Do you believe that mouthy, stupid woman yesterday? I never, that was awful. I wanted to give her a piece of my mind. Her tour was boring. I've never been so bored, and she didn't know when to shut up."

Tommy and I knew it was coming. It was just a matter of time. She didn't want to walk outside and see the seagulls. She didn't want to finish her favorite breakfast. It was over and ruined the moment that woman opened her mouth to Mom.

We returned to our rooms, and she was already packed and pacing. "No pressure, but it's time to go. Are you ready? Yeah, that woman was out of line."

This perfect stranger had cut Mom to the core. Mama didn't know her and would never see her again, and allowed her to take her whole wonderful series of memories away. Nothing would change it. Mom claimed victim status, and that was that.

On the way home, in the car, there were mutterings from the back seat. "She really had it in for me." Tom and I were quiet. There was nothing to say because we knew Mama, and God Himself could not change her mind.

Caretaking is an art form, a delicate dance. I believe we intuitively know when to speak and when it is fruitless.

Tom and I had to realize that we had done the best we could but couldn't change Mom. We can only change our attitude. Sometimes, we have to search our souls, ask honest questions, "Did we do our best?" If so, tune out, let go, and move on. Granted, it is not always easy. Moving on was a tough one for Mama. Weeks later, she would still refer to the rude, ignorant woman.

Recollection

I remember a time with the healing ministry that I was challenged to move on. People were coming to the abbey from all over the world—Canada, Columbia, Brazil, Puerto Rico, Portugal, etc. Some were staying at the abbey. It was, no doubt, a busy time. The sufferings are always with us, and there are so many.

A woman shuffled through the Marian assistants and office personnel; she marched up to my desk and said, "Do you know what you are? A dog and pony show. You are not Jesus. You don't even return messages." Yikes!

I was stunned. I was kind of wishing that Jesus Himself would manifest in person and calm the waters, but I felt, at the time, like He had left me hanging out to dry, and I couldn't make myself disappear.

The attack went straight to ego. Who? Me? What did I do? What had upset her so? I knew I had to get to the heart of the matter, which was simply her frustration at not being able to reach me, and more importantly, she had a very sick son.

It takes a minute to move out of victim status and go to a place where we don't take everything personally. I had a momentary vision of myself as a dog or pony, and my peace and sense of privacy was definitely challenged.

I became Mama! What does she mean? She had a lot of moxie coming in like that. The truth is she loved her son, just as I loved mine. Mine was healthy; hers was not. She was tired, frustrated, and wanted help; she felt she was locked out. It didn't matter that the office was accommodating and the ladies staffing it were lovely volunteers doing the best they could. She could not see through her pain, her fear. We've all been there. She felt abandoned.

There is the nurse who won't let us talk to the doctor. There is the overburdened doctor who is trying to get to all the calls but doesn't. There is the pharmacist who has yet to fill the pain prescription. There is the orthopedist who was called out for surgery at our appointment time. There is the medicine that doesn't work, etc. Also, throw in a fatigue level that doesn't waver. Grab three hours of sleep here and there. Stress! So we don't say what we really mean or if we do, we do not pick and choose words wisely; we attack. Someone has to pay.

We attack when we are threatened. We go for the jugular. We want someone to feel the pain and frustration we're feeling.

Often, we go after the nurturers in our lives. Why? Because they'll take it. We go after the innocents because we catch them off guard and, most probably, they won't respond in anger. We need somebody to listen. We also need forgiveness and understanding—all part of love. We want it even if our approach is wrong. Our victims should be mind readers: don't they know we're in pain?

Adorable Lord, give me discernment. Give me patience. Help me to bypass distorted thinking and know that attacks are a cry for Your help and love. Help me to not judge but to respond in love as you would with compassion and mercy.

As Mom grew sicker and would not acknowledge it, her attacks were more numerous and unsolicited, and forgiveness was not on the table for negotiation. If Mama heard it in her head one way, forgiveness was not an option and letting it go was not even a possibility.

A very dear friend of Mom received a phone call from Mama. It was brief and to the point. "I'm done with you. Don't call me. Don't come to my house anymore!" And then the infamous hang up.

Mom's daughters tried to reason with her. The woman had loved Mama for at least forty years. It made no sense! (Just like the dog and pony story.) We were told it was none of our business and to "butt out!" We did.

I have to ask though, why wasn't this confrontation worthy of discussion, maybe even diffusion? What makes us shut down? What makes us threatened by conversation even with those who love us most? Fear rears its ugly head when least expected, and forgiveness is not in the cards. In a book called *Forgiveness*, Matthew West has a line, an unforgettable line: "It's the hardest thing to give away, the last thing on your mind today. It always goes to those who don't deserve forgiveness."

I have come to realize that unforgiveness binds us, holds us, and keeps us from our God-given mission to love. When I have experienced really challenging times in my life, the first urge is flight. Tom and I have a beautiful waterfront home on a lake. It has served as a peaceful retreat for many years and, also, at times, as a diversion. I remember, specifically, a time in my life that a group of misguided women, together, chose me to target. I had choices: I could return the favor, I had the ammo, or I could think through it. Forgive them and move on.

When I arrived at the lake after this incident, I arrived agitated and annoyed. I went to turn on the TV, and it did not work. Lightning had struck the wires. Think about that. Lightning had struck the wires; it was symbolic. It had struck my wires too.

I believe in signs. I believe they are everywhere and go on all day. So I believed that my God didn't want me to watch the TV at this time. He felt, I believe, that some solitude and prayer were in order.

It is important to "be still and know that I am God" (Psalm 46). This is when we hear His voice. I was able to dismiss the offense, move on, forgive the women, and send them love in prayer. I don't know what became of them or their lives. Their actions were between them and God. He knows what's best for each one. We know that we reap what we sow, and it better be love. That's what we want coming back.

A Season for Everything

We tried to teach Mom meditation. She said, "I can't sit still for that." We talked about the power of prayer. Mom annoyingly said, "Don't preach to me, Ann." She was right. I don't appreciate preachy people. Why would she? Let's see some folks live it! I would be quiet for a while.

Mama did not like God conversations. She would not initiate them or sit for them, not usually. As she became sicker, I would push the envelope a little. I remember a Saturday I brought her lunch and sat down. She had about six books stacked on a little table where I usually sat.

"Take 'em home, Ann. I don't want them."

"You need to lighten up and read some Danielle Steel, Nora Roberts." And I believe she threw John Grisham into the mix. The anger was followed by silence.

I took a breath and said, "What's going on, Mama?"

"Nothing, I'm just tired of this heavy stuff."

I responded, "Did you read it?"

She responded, "Nope, whaddya bring me for lunch?"

I said, "Chicken salad. You didn't like any of them?"

She said again, "Nope" and changed the subject to spring, inviting me to transition with her.

"Ann, when the weather is warmer, I'm going to see this guy I saw on television to fix my back." Mama had now been told on at least three occasions that she had a fracture in her back from a squamous cell cancer that grew and expanded on her spine. She was told that the tumor could possibly be shrunk a little, but not eliminated.

It is significant that Mom was not using the word *cancer*. It had been two years of cancer, and Mom would not call it by name, usually referring to it as a little stiffness.

As caretaker, we ask at what time is it appropriate to call a spade a spade. Do we let her remain in denial or oh so subtly remind her that she's dealing with cancer and maybe there are some other things she'd like to do or talk about?

I would trust my gut, my stomach's reaction, and let it go a little longer. I did this with reservation. And I hauled my little spiritual library home with me.

I would continue to be Mama's advocate though, at times, difficult. I would knock each day, and she would open with "Oh, it's just you" or "Oh, it's just you again." We would see doctors again and again, and she'd tell me I was overdressed or overtipping. She would ask me why I have to talk to everyone. "One day, somebody's going to shoot you!" I thought, *Well then, I won't be talking to everybody and overtipping*.

Mama started eating a mouthful of this and a mouthful of that. She'd be in the mood for just green beans or just mashed potatoes; it varied. I would cook everything, hoping something would stick, something would appeal to her. She'd say, "Ann, I see why all the kids gave you that apron with the Jewish mother on it. You are a food pusher." "Yup, that's me, the Jewish/Catholic mother."

Sweet Jesus, help me to keep *Your* perspective. Help me to keep my sense of humor and always look deeper for You for compassion and understanding. I choose only to see through eyes of love.

As Mom continued to lose weight, she would comment on her clothes bagging. I would suggest we buy some more or alter the ones she liked. She'd say, "Maybe in the spring I'll gain some weight." Spring and warmer weather were her reference points for everything. Did she know, at some level of her mind, that she would complete her journey back to God in the spring?

There is one thing that still stands out in my mind. She asked me repeatedly to hand her the makeup bag. She would redraw her lips and eyebrows repeatedly! She was very concerned about her external appearance.

In the last five days of Mom's life, she had two dramatic falls, one at her home and one at my home, which took her by ambulance to St. Francis Hospital. As she lay on the floor, covered in blood, she asked for her makeup bag. The family didn't know what to make of it. She wanted the outside right.

Mama had a doctor's appointment the previous week. It would be her last, and she felt lousy. I literally supported her as she exited the car and rode up the elevator to Dr. Glenn's office. Mama stopped midway and said, "Ann, how could you let me out like this? I have spots all over my pants! I'm mortified." She had great concern about her outer appearance, but I was to ask on several occasions, "Mom, would you like to see or talk to a priest?" Her comment was "About what?" My response, "I dunno, something, anything." She would also add, "I'm busy. I don't have time."

What did Mom do behind closed doors all day every day? Nobody knows. We do know she liked Lawrence Welk, Archie Bunker, *The Waltons,* Andy Griffith, and VCU basketball. I believe I mentioned that the priest asked Mom at the cemetery after Dad's burial, "What can I do for you?" She responded, "I have to go home and watch Notre Dame football." Family had become used to these comments and responses. We were somewhat anesthetized.

Only now do I ponder what she was thinking. I can honestly say I don't know. Could she be that tough or strong or carefree? I don't think so. I'll never know.

Toward the end of Mama's life, I asked a family friend/priest she loved to call and chat. Maybe Father James had some thoughts. He called me back and said Mama wanted to know what he was up to, and she was cheery and didn't sound sick. I did ask the priest if she had any spiritual questions or concerns. His answer was no.

I've pondered lots of things since her passing. I remember a time preceding Mom's second surgery. The nurses were prepping her when an argument broke out. Mom was using bad language to make her point. "I'm not removing my underwear." The nurse stood her ground. "You can remove it or I will." This fired Mom up as she lectured the nurse about what was necessary and unnecessary. Mom's sense of privacy was off the charts, whether a question of home or her body.

I decided to be silent and watch this debacle play out. I had two thoughts. The first was that Mom might not make it through this very serious surgery, and she was concerned about underpants. Mom was a nurse, and she knew the procedure. Humph. The other nurse could have chosen to calm the then-eighty-nine-year-old woman with high blood pressure and take care of this detail when the pros began anesthesia. Mom went to war, but inevitably she lost this one. She refused every opportunity to talk about cancer, death, dying, or the afterlife, but fought for her underwear.

Sweet Jesus, help me to focus on what matters to You. Help me to remember time is a gift and to spend it wisely. Give me, in Your love and mercy, the gift of discernment.

Two Is Company, Three Is a Crowd

Mom had, throughout my life, consistently issued invitations to part of the family, but rarely all three sisters and their husbands and children simultaneously. Christmas was a rare exception.

If there was a rift in the family, Mom was quick to take sides and isolate the offender of her choice. She would deliver a rough message, hang up on you, and then call for Christmas dinner. She would declare an end to friction and issue the coveted invitation to Christmas Eve dinner. Everything would be forgiven; there would be no discussion of it. It was simply over, and all would pretend it never happened. This reminds me of her cancer. She would ignore it, bury thoughts of it, and not discuss it, but it was spreading, and it would not go away. It would take her life.

Each daughter waited month upon month for a special conversation, where we could all talk about important issues. Each wanted to know what she was feeling or thinking. We wanted to help and to support her. But mind reading was not our strong suit. All we could do was guess based on her life patterns.

We desperately wanted her to share a special part of her, to hear what mattered in her long life, what memories were treasured, what she was learning from her suffering and cancer journey, what she could pass along to us to help our lives, what thoughts she would like to pass along to her children and grandchildren. There was nothing.

I never knew her favorite color. Maybe green. I never knew what she really treasured, what made her hysterically laugh, if and when she prayed, and what she prayed for. I never knew exactly what she thought about an afterlife, what she knew or felt definitively about her God. She told me once that she decided to pray ten Hail Marys. "It was too hard to pray the whole rosary. All that repetition."

She never talked about prayer but made sure each of her girls received the sacraments and attended Mass on Sundays. She sent us to Catholic schools, just as her mother sent her and her siblings to Catholic schools, to receive the sacraments of Baptism, Penance, Eucharist, Confirmation, and, later, Marriage.

There were no spiritual discussions of faith, however, in our home. When I asked about Extreme Unction (the sacrament of the sick) when a friend of mine passed at a young age, the only comment was "Ann, you wear your heart on your sleeve. If you're going to that funeral, don't cry. Be a source of strength. You're way too sensitive. Knock it off!"

I determined, at a young age, that crying was for the weak. Mom's eyes would fill sometimes during her cancer journey. I would reach out to hold and touch her. Her comment, "Knock it off. I'm fine." It's almost as if she would catch herself, do self-talk: "Don't feel." The stern, solemn look would reappear. I knew intuitively that there was no approaching her.

It was in Yugoslavia, where the Marian apparitions were taking place, that I finally received permission to cry. I had felt the presence of Mary the Queen of Peace. I was totally overwhelmed with peace and joy; I felt removed from this earth. I cried like a baby and, when approached by a priest, covered my eyes. Father Slavko said, "Never be ashamed of your tears. They're healing and cleansing. They are a gift from God."

This marked an epiphany in my life. Since, I've cried and cried an ocean of tears. I cry when I'm overwhelmed with joy or sadness. I cry at the birth of a baby. I cry at Wounded Warrior commercials. I cry at graduations.

What's different? Me. I know our mental computers are full of recorded instances in our lives—bits and pieces and not sorted out with any logic or spirituality. These instances pop up to threaten and haunt us when on the verge of joy or success.

One of mine was from childhood and said, "Don't cry. It's a sign of weakness." My soul determined otherwise. We do not have to accept negative and destructive messages. We have, in every moment of our lives, choices. It is not about what other people think; it is about a higher calling of the heart, and it's personal. It is about God saying, "You perform for me and me alone." With God, all things are possible.

I've had to undo lots of programming. I'm sure Mama struggled with it. We are victims of victims, and we can only give what we have been given. With God's help, we move beyond and become productive human beings.

Jesus, help me to hear one voice—Yours!

Love Is All There Is!

Nothing, absolutely nothing, else heals. Knowing this and having been blessed with many mystical and miraculous experiences, I knew that only love could influence Mom's journey and my soul's journey.

I would give it all I had; nothing less would do. There were times I'd go home on the pity pot, thinking I was just lost. I would feel irritated with her. She would berate nurses, doctors, telephone repair people, and well-intentioned associates and family members—everyone who was trying to alleviate her fear and frustrations. I believe, as Vincent Benet said, "Life is not lost by dying. Life is lost minute by minute, day by dragging day in all the small uncaring ways."

I would spend hours scheduling appointments. One of these was for an MRI. Mom decided it didn't work for her. I rescheduled, and at that time, she announced she wasn't going if it wasn't an open bore unit. She waited until the second scheduling to tell me she was claustrophobic. I cancelled that appointment and scheduled one at the open bore facility, which was north of the river. She wanted that changed because she did not want to go north of the James River. I did not change it and, between my husband and me, spent the entire day tracking the composition of her eyelid insert to see if she could even have an MRI. The doctor's office had no info, note to doctor. "If you insert it, then keep the company name, model number, and whether it is pure gold or not. Keep that info handy, please!" Mom's hard to get appointment was scheduled for early morning. My Tommy tracked the insert to Canada via an associate at St. Mary's

Hospital. The MRI approval came electronically at 5:00 p.m. before the MRI. Only love persists in the face of all drama. That love was my husband, who lives it!

Tom also held Mom's foot during the procedure for security. When it was over, Mom said, "Let's eat and go home."

We dropped her off to "I know you must be tired of hanging with this old lady."

I kept thinking, *Can't she see how much we love her? Does she really define herself as a bother and old lady?* I kept telling her how much we loved her, but she never really acknowledged it. I couldn't see that she felt it. That made me sad. Without love, we are lost, incomprehensible to ourselves. I must continue to try.

I believe Mother Teresa said, "Never, never quit." I would see this journey through to the end, and the end was not far off.

Sweet Jesus, give me the strength and courage to do Your will, not mine. Transform my doubts and troubles into miracles. I know tomorrow is not my enemy because You are with me.

I needed to remember the scripture, "For as he [or she] thinketh in his [her] heart, so is he [she]" Proverbs 23:7. Our thoughts determine our success in life, and they either invite the Holy Sprit's help or contribute to our destruction. When our hearts are open, we choose to love and joy follows.

Leon Bloy said, "The infallible sign of God's presence is joy." Our great saints were joyful even in their sufferings. St. Francis was always singing. His joy was contagious even amid His sufferings.

I wanted Mom to experience joy. I would pray for this. Mother Teresa told her sisters to be of good cheer. She said, "A cheerful sister is like a net that catches souls for God."

I found it interesting that the father of modern atheism, Nietzsche, who claimed that God is dead, said, "If you want me to believe in a redeemer, show me people who look like they're redeemed." Where's the joy?

Times are terrible, but we all have so many blessings, so many things we take for granted, to be joyful about—home, food, children, jobs, waking to a new day, etc. We need to wear our joy because it's contagious! There will always be suffering intermingled with our joy, but we need to make joy and God our goal.

One of my favorite reads is Kahlil Gibran. He writes profoundly about joy and suffering. It is the Holy Spirit who helps us balance and find the joy even in suffering. I will be joy whenever I am with the sick and suffering. I will smile and end my days with Mom with big hugs and a smile no matter what. I will try harder to represent God more consistently with joy when I believe my name is D-Ann, (no, not Diane, but Dammit, Ann!) I will smile. I will elicit more joy—if it kills me (chuckle). Remember, I'm the melodramatic one.

Lord, I summon with total commitment and sincere heart my gift of joy!

I have funny, entertaining, and joy-filled friends. They would pitch in with Mama. It became a challenge to provide Mom with joy.

Jill and I entered Krim Point wearing hysterical Halloween hats, singing, laughing, and joking. We had a hat for Mom, but she didn't want to mess up her hair. Jill and I kept smiling. We stepped up our act; we showed up at Christmas with Christmas hats adorned with lights and bling and sleds and Santa. We loved our hats. This time, we had a plan. We also had a hat for Mom. We wore them to the Commonwealth Club in Richmond. Mom left hers in the car. We kept smiling and took Mom to see the big gingerbread house at the Jefferson Hotel, and we kept smiling. Holidays emit an automatic joy; and we did get a smile from Mom. She did love Jill. Jill is from New York. Mom has relatives in New York, and I was born there.

CoCo is Irish and a Yankee, and so was mom. Mom loved the Irish. She also loved Yankees. The first question out of her mouth was "Where are you from? You sound like a Yankee." No matter that she spent sixty years in Virginia. Mom also loved CoCo. The three of us would go to lunch weekly unless Mom didn't feel like it or there was a scheduling conflict.

One particular lunch date day, Mom called early to say she wanted to skip it. She was feeling poorly. I said we'd come by and check on her. At which time she said, "Nope, don't come. I want to rest. Don't bother me."

YOU CAN'T DRIVE YOUR CAR TO YOUR OWN FUNERAL

Somewhat concerned, CoCo and I decided to go to lunch and then go check on Mom. We headed down the pike for French onion soup in a shopping center. We finished and were getting in CoCo's car when CoCo started giggling and said, "Hey, isn't that your Mom?" Yup, sure enough, she was pulling out of Taco Bell in the adjacent shopping center. You couldn't miss that little car with the license plate PRRFEC. Don't ask, I have no idea why she chose PRRFEC. I have no idea why she didn't choose to endure our charming company. Teasing CoCo, I said, "Are we boring?" We just laughed, followed her down the pike to Target, and waited her out to make sure she was still OK. We decided we'd humiliate her if she saw us, so we went about our business. Yes, it's true. Our date dumped us. We would never address this with her. It would remain a sister-friend secret, and we would smile about it. Mom traded us for a burrito.

There was another interesting date day with a twist. CoCo and I stopped by the house for a visit. Mama did not invite us in. Believe it! It's true. She said, "I was on my way out." She also said, "Hang on" and went to get her purse. She said, "You wanna go to the Peking and pick up some chicken and broccoli for me?" CoCo and I traveled to the nearby shopping center and made the purchase. We would, of course, pay for it ourselves. We returned from our little errand. Mom took the food, said thanks, and left CoCo and me on the porch. She said that she was having company that evening and the Chinese food would suffice.

You had to laugh. It was funny. It was my mama. As Abbot Benedict always said, "Love her where she is."

Lord, please help me to see the humor in life. Keep me smiling for the love of Thee!

Side note: I have another friend, a little more fragile. She never met Mama. One day, I was bragging about my friend. Mom interrupted, saying, "Is she the one who doesn't like . . ."

I said, "Yup."

"I never liked her," said Mama.

You've got to laugh. You can't make this stuff up. The stories are sitcom material.

Keeping Up with Mama

I was generally concerned about Mama self-medicating. "I found this in the medicine chest. I'm gonna try it."

I left her one night to go home and let our dog out. I advised Mama to wait for my return for her medication. She went to my deceased father's medicine chest and decided to try one of his meds.

I returned, and she couldn't or wouldn't recall what she'd taken. This would happen more than once.

Note to self: When someone passes away, remove all medications. Also, if you are concerned about overmedicating, there are little marked pill cases that you can fill for morning and evening. These may be purchased at any pharmacy.

It should be noted here that some days Mom would opt to skip her medication and have a Manhattan. That was her own mother's drink. Mama would always say, "And don't forget the cherry juice."

My mama journal is full of stories. Going back through some is extremely painful. Looking at them on paper brings to the surface a lot of emotions I would never let myself feel or own. I was so busy taking care of and trying to uplift and please Mom that I realize now that I had a "Yes, Mama-itis." And a serious soul-searching has begun.

I have always had an unrealistic identity attachment to both my mother and father. While the two of them had a challenging relationship, I always subconsciously thought I could fix it. If I won one more honor, one more title, one more prize, I could make them happy, and that happiness would spill over to me. I had to be perfect. Abbot Benedict asked me one day, "Oh, so you're God now?"

Yes, I'm the oldest and the representative of the typical pattern that goes with this—the "Yes, Mama-itis" caretaker. I always wanted to please her and everyone. I thought my mission was to make everyone happy. I had a gift of gab from a small age. I knew in fourth grade I would pursue television. I love people; I love interviewing, getting inside their heads to find out what they care about, what they value, how they choose to make the world a better place, what and how they think.

I was privileged to interview scientists, world leaders like Abba Eban, spiritual leaders like the Dalai Lama, move stars, the list was endless. I did documentaries and network commercials. I could not believe that I was paid for the exciting television career I enjoyed. I was honored for my work and had large opportunities that I was to ignore. My agent, Bill Cooper, in New York found positions, and I would pass on them.

My mama said repeatedly in my life, "Ann, you have a glamour hang-up. You've got to get real." I thought I was real, but Mom's words would have an enormous impact on me, and I would walk away from TV.

I had a temporary license to teach, and I loved children. I taught the wee ones at Chalkley and loved it. I would later teach senior English (an elective) at St. Gertrude High School in Richmond, where I had been president of the student body in 1964. I loved it and was voted graduation speaker by the senior class. I also taught a class in communications, lectured at several other schools, and was recognized for my work.

I remember visiting home and Mom saying, "Teaching? You're a natural-born star. You're an entertainer. Why would you teach? You don't make sense."

I never realized, until now, the impact her comments had on me. I wasn't living my best life, but rather Mama's feelings of the week. I just wanted to please her and, in doing so, became Mom's manipulation project. I was remembering a scene from *Runaway Bride*, where Julia Roberts is trying to decide who she is and what she really likes. She fixes eggs Benedict, scrambled eggs, poached eggs, and fried eggs and mindfully samples each and makes her own decision as to what eggs she likes best. She started with eggs and expanded to life experiences.

We are all products of the environment in which we grew up. We are all products of the belief system that was instilled in us. Our egos do not acknowledge reason or discussion. Ego records events without explanation. It haunts us for a lifetime. Our most profound thoughts are traced back to our lives with Mom and Dad. They're all in the memory bank.

Most of us spent years with Mom and Dad. They unconsciously gave us our thought patterns, right and wrong, politics, culture, likes and dislikes, religion bias, etc. It is all inside us. Our most formative years were with our parents or those who raised us, taught us, and, hopefully, nurtured us.

This explains why, often, our minds hold us slaves. These recorded images often keep us from living the lives that God intended for us. In my computer are such statements as: "It's very important what the neighbors think," "You are way too sensitive. You wear your heart on your sleeve," "You are way too sentimental," "You have to toughen up," "Strong people don't cry," "Crying is a sign of weakness," "Doctors are gods and not to be challenged," "Be careful what you say. People might not like it," "You're a dreamer, get real," "Everybody argues," and "You never share what goes on in the family. Families keep their secrets private."

As a teenager, I thought we don't even know our neighbors; we come in alone and go out alone (with our God). Why is it important what the neighbors think? Particularly if we are speaking the truth? Why is it bad to be sentimental, caring, or loving? Why is crying bad? I feel like I am acknowledging my emotions, my feelings. Is it bad to feel? Why are doctors separate and apart from us? They are human; we pay them for their educated guesses and their skills. They make mistakes like the rest of us. There is no difference!

What about "everybody argues?" <u>No,</u> they don't. How would Mom and Dad know about everybody? Did they take a poll? I don't think so. I found that in my house growing up, the word *everybody* was used to convince us that a certain behavior was normal rather than dysfunctional. In our home, to make any point valid, one said,

"Everybody says" or "Everyone believes" this or that. I frankly believe a lot of people have different views, beliefs, thoughts, and values. I have been privileged to meet some.

The real epiphany in my life came when I literally saw the one I prayed to since third grade, the one I asked daily at the altar in St. Bridget's to send someone to love me forever, and I would give that love back to the world.

I saw the Virgin Mary, and none of us can deny what is in our experience. I would never deny her! I was told through the visionary Nancy Fowler that I was being given an extraordinary gift of healing, which would bear itself out. This experience is shared in detail in my second book, *Wake Up, America*.

I was humbled, emotional, scared, and, at the time, wanted to hide. I couldn't. If God wants it, nothing stops it. People were healed, stories traveled; network news and TV picked it up and, of course, front-page stories at home in Virginia.

My parents refused to talk about this. It was much easier to acknowledge a TV personality. I saw less and less of them by their choice. They were embarrassed. Meantime, the sensitivity and tears were being used by God to alleviate suffering among His children. I felt blessed, privileged, and humbled to be used by God. The old debater in me might have judged me. "Wow! This is weird." I know some did judge me, and I didn't care. I was making spiritual progress.

For the first time, it didn't matter that my parents were embarrassed. My husband wasn't and my children weren't. When you have a profound, personal, and intimate experience with God. His grace is so overwhelming that if the whole world stood against you, it wouldn't matter. I wanted only to do His will and to be His broom, wherever He chose to use me. Because of Him and His beautiful Mother, I was free. I would cry with the sick, pray with them, and just love and learn from them. They have been, and remain, my greatest teachers—teachers of courage, humility, strength, faith, gratitude, and love.

The wounded healer would face her greatest challenge yet in her own home, on her own turf, and with her own mother, and more lessons were to be learned and processed. It was to be a journey of a different kind—a journey of spirit.

A Unique Solution

The journey of spirit takes place within each soul where we find real freedom. Freedom lies in love that releases pain and unforgiveness and allows complete surrender to His thoughts, His will, and His heart.

There are those, myself included, that say we are seeking to become more spiritual beings. Is it possible that we are trying to become more human? Pilgrims on a journey to discover humanity in all its richness and fullness. We have, however, misguided manuals that emanate more from the head than the heart and heads not our own.

Jesus came to fulfill the law of love—love God and your neighbor as self. This is the unique solution for people strangling in fear.

Granted, fear has many faces: global war, suicide, homelessness, violence, crime, and a suffering that begins to develop in infancy, shaped and developed by everything that has been said to us and everything that has happened to us. We can conjure it in an instant. We then experience anger, resentment, sadness, despair—all born of fear. We make it real! Each day, we choose our heaven or our hell. We do it with woulds, coulds, and shoulds. We do it with jealousy, anger, and unforgiveness. As we create our personal hell, we are creating societal hell, one person at a time.

Negativity originates in fear. "I'm not enough, so I cannot allow you to be enough." Negativity is not only cancerous but also contagious. Just as war comes from collective hostility, so then peace comes from love, which begins with self.

None of us can give what we do not have in our own experience. So we must risk the inner journey and rid ourselves of sick thought. God has said He will not forsake us; He will not leave us orphans.

Through the life and death of Jesus, death became subject to the power of life. Christ's death and resurrection is at the heart of our faith. No one can save us from death or suffering. Our hope is Jeshua (God who saves) (Judges 3:5).

Christ's resurrection embraces each man and places each of us on the cusp of hope. The question that remains is, have we lost our understanding of Christ's vision? Is He not the light that shines in the darkness? God so loved the world that He gave His only begotten Son that we might have life to the fullest.

We have all been given what we need for a happy life. The problem lies in how to use what we've been given. We must first accept the premise that finding spiritual happiness is our life's purpose. Also accept that you and I determine our happiness, not what is going on around us and not what someone else thinks you should do or not do.

We must interpret what is sent to our minds. We must commit to truth. I suggest we can often self-talk our way into misery. We do this by setting others up as judge and jury over major decisions in our lives. We descend into hell by accepting others' negative messages and incorporating them in our mental computers.

We have already established that ego cannot discern truth. Why do we trust other people's egos? Why do we not trust ourselves, our choices, our hearts?

Each person, including family members, have their own issues, truths, biases, and motives. Who knows you better than you?

I would suggest many want to please parents, those who gave us the gift of life. In the process, often boundaries are lost. We have been taught to honor thy father and thy mother, but what does that mean? It does not mean sacrificing our dreams, goals, mission, and/or peace.

I believe that we are called to live authentic lives. We are not copies; we are originals. We, each of us, have a mission unique to us, our gifts and talents.

My gifts have always been people, journalism, and television. I have received numerous awards for each. This is not about bragging, for all gifts come from God.

My question for me is, why would I walk away from what I love, have a passion for, and have been honored for? There is a profound dynamic at work here and deserves discussion for all of us.

Our thoughts can be traced back to childhood and the people responsible for us—our caretakers, usually parents. They clothe us, feed us, and shelter us. Some, hopefully many, nurture our spirit. Isn't it accurate that we owe them a debt of gratitude, if only for basic life-sustaining necessities? Where do we set boundaries?

I believe we intuitively know when our ideas, (self-determined) goals, and hopes are compromised. I also believe that because of the reward system from our youth—the good girl, bad girl syndrome—we master people pleasing (*Let It Go – Exploring and Escaping the 'Good Girl' Syndrome* by Margaret Manning).

I can honestly say I always wanted to make Mama and Daddy happy and, sometimes, to my own detriment. I would contend that we all carry massive baggage from our childhood environment. It becomes part of us. We must learn discernment.

How many vote the way Mom and Dad voted? How many dislike the same people Mom and Dad disliked? Children live what they learn. If Mom and Dad are labelers, do we label? If they were fighters and name-callers, how do you handle confrontations? Peacefully addressing issues or screaming and with phone hang-ups, and name-calling? Words like *stupid, lazy, slob, liar, fat*, etc., stay with us for a lifetime.

I cite the example of Martha Friedman, author and scholar, when writing her book *Overcoming the Fear of Success*. Instead, she wrote "overcoming success." Where did that come from? You know (Warner books).

When I announced that I wanted to transition from radio to television, the response at home was "You have a good job. How are you going to do that? You don't know anybody. Everybody wants to be on TV. Be happy with what you have, Ann."

I could have stopped there, but being an adventure seeker, I wanted to know more and explore more and grow more. I went to work for Van Cantfort at WAVY-TV in Tidewater, Virginia, cohosting *Compass*, a morning show. How do we know what we can do if we don't try? Isn't it possible that God puts a desire in our hearts and for His purpose? I've said that our lives are tapestries, one segment built upon the next, an interwoven fabric taking us to the next adventure. I pursued TV.

I learned to think before I speak and to speak mindfully. I learned that I had an opportunity to help people using media. I learned poise on camera.

One example of using media for greater purpose is the Virginia Rehabilitation Award I was given for getting a bus stop moved for the handicapped at the Virginia Home. The adults and children in the Norfolk area wanted an elephant for their zoo. I was able to start a green stamp movement to secure the elephant through media.

We are only limited by our own imaginations, the judgments of others that we choose to own, and by our own fictitious beliefs.

How many times do we procrastinate? I'll do that after I have my second child. I'll do that when I'm a little older. I'll wait to see when they think the time is right. Listen to your own heart.

All we have is now, this moment, not even the next moment. Yesterday is gone, and tomorrow is an unknown. Time is a gift. Ask seniors who don't know what happened to their lives—gone in an instant. Their lives are full of woulds, shoulds, and could haves, but they didn't! And they can't get it back; none of us can. When it's gone, it's gone. Every moment is an opportunity. Make a choice to live an authentic life. Make it your own. Choose to love and live. Find joy in each day. "Life is an adventure or nothing at all" as Helen Keller said, and joy is the infallible presence of God.

There can be no joy without forgiveness. This one is often tough, I know. I also acknowledge that unforgiveness enslaves us. We do not forgive to help the offender. We forgive for us. It is the gift we give ourselves. I discovered a long time ago that when I carry anger, resentment, and judgment, I am miserable. We cannot be the best we can be carrying this garbage around. It tarnishes our souls.

I found that imagining the offenders as small innocent children dancing in a meadow helped me to remember their innocence and openness. We don't know what happens to people in their life journeys. We are not privy to their thoughts and sufferings, but I tend to think that they have temporarily forgotten who they are. If they have forgotten that they are children of God, how can they remember that you are also a child of God?

We must let go! There need not be a face-to-face. Just let go and visualize them going into the distance, disappearing with the Lord. Wish them well. It makes forgiveness easier to think that life is a remembering and a forgetting. We are all human, and at some given time, we have all offended someone. We must give what we desire to receive—love and forgiveness. When we forgive, we set ourselves free. It is about us.

I was convinced a long time ago that Mama's hang-ups and long verbal accusations came from pain. If she misinterpreted something or heard it the way she defined it in her mind in any given moment, and based on her mood at the time, she learned to attack. The attacks became a pattern of learned behavior.

I thought the heart attack, cancer, and cellulitis would make her slow down, think, and maybe change; but her fear controlled her until the end. I know my sweet Jesus knows her heart, her pain, and her sorrow. Jesus's love covers all.

As I mentioned, the week before Mom passed, she fell twice in one day. This was the beginning of the end. My sister stopped by Mom's home and found her on the floor. At this point in Mom's journey, she was dead weight. My sister could not get her up. The dialogue continued for a while, and my sister realized Mom was still in control. She did not want anyone outside the family in the house. My sister had no choice but to call a neighbor.

By the time I arrived, Mom was livid and sitting in her chair across the room. She looked at me and said, "Why are you here?" Without taking offense, I said, "Mom, I heard you took a fall. What happened?" Mom's response was terse, "No big deal. Back off, Ann."

YOU CAN'T DRIVE YOUR CAR TO YOUR OWN FUNERAL

My sister and I conferenced outside in the yard, and a decision was made that Mom would come to my house and spend the night and maybe a couple of days.

I was entertaining for the week. Our granddaughter, Kendall, eleven years old, was spending her break with Grandma and Grandpa. I would double-team Mama, and Tommy would tend to Kendall.

The Last Meal

Left to right: Maddie, Chase, Jack, Kendall

No sooner than we got Mama settled at the farm, we realized it was past 6:30. Mama said she was hungry and could eat some veal parmesan, her favorite dish. We were excited that Mom had an appetite after the trauma of her day. Tom went to Candelas and brought veal and spaghetti home for everyone. I had spumoni ice cream in the freezer. We'd have a party and watch the NCAA basketball tournament.

Mom, to this point, had a tiny appetite and had gone from 178 to 116 pounds. She would eat a bite of this or two or three green beans here and there. It was heartbreaking.

This night was different, stunning, and referenced in the hospice manuals under last weeks of life. Mom ate a large portion of spaghetti, veal parmesan, and ice cream. Very unusual.

Kendall had fixed a large bowl of spumoni for Mama. I didn't believe she would eat any of it. She ate all of it. It was so wonderful to see Mama smile and enjoy her meal and her great-granddaughter.

Shortly after, we tucked Mama in our bed and gave her a cowbell. We left the light at the far end of the room lighted for her. I would sleep on the floor at the foot of her bed. We had a porta-potty next to our bed for Mama.

About three or four in the morning, I got up to check on Kendall, who was sleeping upstairs. I asked Mama if she needed to get up or excuse herself. The answer was "No, Ann. You should go and sleep with your husband."

I had not even ascended the steps and I heard, "Help!" Just a tiny, weak, soft help. I went flying back into my room to find Mom on the floor and covered in blood. I was shaking and frightened. I called Tom and an ambulance.

This was Mom's second fall in twenty-four hours. Why didn't she ring the bell? Why did she get up after telling me she did not need to?

Mass confusion reigned. Kendall was up. The ambulance had arrived. Tom was filling out some papers for Mom. Mom was asking for her make-up bag. She needed her new lipstick.

Yes, Mom was flat on her back on the floor, covered in blood, and was drawing eyebrows and applying lipstick.

I am answering questions about Mom's health, and Mama was correcting me and giving specific information to the medical team, complete with names and dates. She was sharp as a tack.

We were in the ambulance together headed for St. Francis again. I had to ride up front. I kept asking, "You OK, Mama?" "Yup" came from the back.

I cannot begin to count our times at St. Francis in a three-year period. This would be the last time. They stitched Mama's head and wanted to send her home. The sisters conferenced with my friend CoCo. CoCo had a great deal of experience with home health and hospice in her job as a social worker. We knew, as never before, that Mama could not be left alone even for short periods. She was very weak though still fighting and scrappy.

It just wasn't safe anymore. Mama would require constant care, and remember, she'd fired home health twice already.

We had to make an important decision.

The three of us stood at the foot of the hospital bed feeling very much like conspirators must feel. Calls were made quickly, and decisions were definitively made. The hospital was ready to release Mama—*again!*

I could not be at Mama's house 24-7. Mama did not want to move in with us. She insisted on her independence. This was no longer possible—not healthy and not safe. The answer was *no*, but who would tell her? Not me!

Betty just came out with it while I froze in my tracks.

"Mom, we've hired hospice. We can't manage by ourselves anymore."

She did it—dropped the bomb. That's the way it felt to me. Mom who always called the shots, Mom who had PRRFEC for her license plate, Mom who had her permit renewed at ninety-one, the mom who always got her way was told, "You can't stay alone anymore."

We waited, all three of us, in silence until the response came, "Oh no, I'm not paying for this. We're not doing this!" Then the voice from the pitiful three, "Yes, you are. We must. We need help."

This was followed by the toughest look you ever saw, head wrapped, arms folded. The look was *anger*.

"Ann, I'm sure you have some place to be. Go! CoCo, I'm sure you have to be going. Betty, you need to be back at the hospital."

Yes, Mom was dismissing the team. She needed to process, and I know she didn't want us to see her crack. She was so private and tough, but this was literally, for Mama, the end. She did say as if to double-check herself, "Someone will be with me *all* the time?" Yes, Mama.

The woman who remained behind locked doors for two years was no longer free—no more lunches out, no more car driving. Mama would never, again, get out of bed. She quit that day at St. Francis.

It's as if Mama knew she had sacrificed, unwillingly, all control. She never wanted hospice. We'd never uttered the word in her presence until that morning at the hospital when important decisions had to be made.

Mama lay in a hospital bed in her living room from that day until her death five days later, April 2, 2015. She uttered only a few words, very few. For the most part, Mom did it her way. There was no nursing home, no assisted care, and she had in-home hospice for only five days. God is good!

I still wonder what Mama thought those last days. Could she forgive us? Did we need forgiving? To take anyone's independence and freedom is awful, but to know what freedom meant to Mom and press forward was very difficult.

We all knew that the falls were becoming a pattern. We also knew that we were frightened of moving her and possibly creating more pain for her. And the truth is that we could no longer lift her, and she was too weak to assist.

I would sit with her those last days and pray the rosary for her peace. She was able to mouth, "I love you" the first two days at home, and then she slept and slept until she passed into eternity.

I was numb. The last three years were a blur. My dad had died suddenly and unexpectedly. There was no time to grieve. Mom had been in and out of St. Francis with cancer, cellulitis, a heart attack, more cancer, and then the falls. I myself had been in the hospital while all this was going on.

Fireworks

The summer of '13 was most challenging. Our family usually spent June and July at our summer place at Lake Gaston—skiing, swimming, boating, fishing, grilling, and just being together with lots of laughter, four grandchildren, four dogs, great movies, and good food.

This summer was surreal. I was waiting for a hip replacement, alternating between a wheelchair and a rollator. Mama was very sick and I was functioning, but heartbroken. To make matters worse, July 4 would see fireworks like no other. I still wake up nights thinking about it and wondering what my God was trying to teach me. I really thought He had given up on *obedience*. I remember Father Donald from Maryland saying, "The angels take Tylenol when you wake up in the morning, Ann Marie." I guess he was indicating that "I am a project."

The Fourth of July was a beautiful day. I had a visit to Mom's with flowers. The sky was blue, and mystical shapes danced among the puffy cotton candy clouds. I was sentimental thinking about Dad and his sacrifices for America at Guadalcanal. He was a proud Marine Raider. I thought about my son, Chip, and his sacrifices as a captain and Special Ops Marine Raider team leader. I pondered about his work in Ramadi, Fallujah, Southeast Asia, and I thanked God that my guys returned home to their families.

I was content and thanking God for all my blessings. We take so much for granted. I looked around and decided I would go outside and pick gardenias from the garden. They are my very favorite flowers. I had, however, been told to rest to prepare for the evening celebration. There would be no bands or barbeques for me. There would, however, be big-time fireworks!

I spent the Fourth of July at Johnston-Willis Hospital. I had a high white cell count, and red lumps covered my entire body. I had experienced a serious, toxic allergic response to something that bit me in my garden. My breathing was interrupted. It was terrifying!

I have been in intensive care many times—too many times—but I can't remember ever previously struggling for air; it is indescribable and the fear that accompanies it is beyond the pale. It is the only moment in my life that I seriously considered letting go for me and my family that I love. They have been to hell and back with me over and over. This was different. What did this? A spider? A snake? An allergy to antibiotics? Hydrocodone reaction from hip pain? What?

Quitting would be so easy. Just let go. Fear is paralyzing, overwhelming; it can take the best part of us if we allow it. I would self-talk. What does God want? Who will care for Mama?

July 5 found me still here, but back in the hospital. There were so many medications and heart monitors going off in the room and in the hall. Nurses couldn't understand my very low blood pressure. They were in and out with steroid injections, insulin injections, Pepcid injections, antibiotic injections, antihistamine injections—puzzled looks and confusion! Fifteen doctors, conflicting opinions, more guesses, more tests, more consults, and more doctors.

I must be imagining this, but my tears are real and taste salty. "Oh my gosh, what about Mama?" I have to get well. I have a hip surgery; it's a week away. I was feeling desolate.

The hip surgery was cancelled. It was almost a year that I was hobbling with my rollator before I acquired my robotic hip. I couldn't think about that. There was Mama to consider.

I pondered Cardinal Newman's mediation on suffering.

"God has created me to do a service, a definite service, one He has committed to no one but me. I have a mission. I am a link in a chain. I shall do good work—His work. I will trust Him. I can't be thrown away. If I am sick, my sickness will serve Him. He does nothing in vain. He may allow me to feel desolate, make my spirits sink, and hide my future, but He knows what He is about. I will serve Him!"

ANN MARIE HANCOCK

Chip (our son) and Mom

I prayed for a long time and then prayed some more.

Sweet Jesus, when the burden is way beyond my strength, lift it. Help me to accept your will. Don't let me wallow in an ocean of useless self-pity. It serves no one.

Let me choose love, courage, faith, and hope. Help me to ponder your passion and suffering for me, your lonely walk to the cross, betrayed by those you love, still love. Help me to come out of me and fly to you, the source of all hope, love, strength, and goodness. You are Jeshua, the God who saves. Save me!

I thought a lot about Mom while in and out of the hospital. I had a flood of thoughts as we do when we are brought to our knees. Why does it take crisis or tragedy to make us think about what really matters? Nevertheless, it is clear that God is trying to get our attention.

In the midst of Mom's crisis, I was in crisis. I believe that God allowed me to share some of her fear and her thoughts. I felt more compassion and more love than I thought possible. I pondered the blessings in my life—my husband, my children, Cori, Faith, Chip, and my incredible grand-children. My mind wandered to a card that I kept from my son, Chip. The card is entitled A Son Remembers.

It's just a kitchen table, much worse for years of wear, with memories in each scratch and stain from all that happened there. The paint that never would come off, a scissor nick or two. The dent where something heavy dropped, a bump, a dried-up place, the scratch left by the cookie sheet, the surface worn and faded where hands were held, grace was said, candles lit, elbows propped, and countless stories traded. It doesn't show the teardrops, and it has not voice to tell the secrets revealed and joys shared, but those are there as well. Life was secure around that kitchen table. Life was happy and secure, and my heart will feel that love as long as memories endure.

I treasure our children. They are all different, all unique. Chip is very humble; he is tall, very kind, very smart, but also private. He brought his whole Marine platoon back from a 2006 Ramadi tour of duty in one piece, an incredible feat that he takes no credit for. As a captain, Chip was a Special Ops team leader. He was moved by 9/11 and wanted to do his part. He is now a health care attorney with Hancock, Daniel, and Johnson, P. C. Tommy, Chip's dad, developed this law specialty in the United States with a handful of others more than forty years ago.

Faith is my Irish rose. Her ice-blue eyes sparkle. She would give you the shirt off her back. She is a total giver, and she is the child I wasn't supposed to have after losing her sister, Stacy, to hyaline membrane disease. Faith loves children and teaches little ones at her childhood alma mater in Richmond.

Cori is my oldest. She is the bravest and most courageous woman I know. Her masters is in counseling, and she too works with children. Cori has had multiple sclerosis for many years. I have never heard her complain. She falls and she gets up. She has had numerous sufferings, not the least of which is she cannot run with her own children. Mike Krzyzewski, Duke coach, compared Cori to Michael Jordan at an MS dinner in North Carolina. She has inspired so many everywhere she goes, always smiling. She is my inspiration.

I have often wondered what inspired Mama. She never said. I wonder if she was proud of her girls. I wonder what she loved and thought about.

It is incredible that we can live with someone half of our lives and honestly say we have no clue as to what they believe about anything—God, politics, life, goals, loves, hobbies?

Lessons

What I can say is that my mama was very courageous and very strong. I know her mom was also private. Grandma never talked about feelings. She was a product of the depression and watched her pennies. Mom was a product of Grandma, but also World War II. Mom was a navy nurse. She never talked about that or her feelings about the war, what she saw, or what she did.

If there was a big blow up in the family, it was never discussed. There would be the phone call, the hang-up, and the two or three months of silence. There was never, ever an apology. It was business as usual and the inevitable move on. We did learn to move on.

I thank God every day for sending me the gentlest, brightest, and wisest man I have ever known—my husband. I met him when I was a teen. He had distinguished himself even then. My mother did concede this one and referenced him as St. Thomas.

Tommy taught me how to fight—you talk about issues. Sometimes you agree, sometimes not, but it's all OK. Disciplinary situations with our children took place in the bedroom where consensus would be reached, and a united front was presented. There was no spanking, no hitting, no name-calling. We did time-outs before they were vogue.

Tommy's mom lived with us after Mr. Hancock passed on. She never raised her voice, and she never said an unkind word about anyone. She was saintly in her demeanor, and I adored her as did our children.

She taught love by her example. She was selfless, service oriented, and kind beyond expression. I know God sent her to me to show me what is possible with His grace. TeTe was extremely gentle and spiritual. There was never an inconvenient time for her, and she never judged anyone.

Tommy and I took care of her at our home for several years with her Parkinson's and Alzheimer's disease. It was only the last few months of her life that she needed outside care. The children and I could and would talk to her about everything, and we'd talk for hours while sitting on her bed. She never judged and always suggested prayer when we were troubled.

I remember something she said two days before she passed on. I asked her if she was scared and held her hand. She said, "I wish I could know for sure what's there." She also asked for God's forgiveness for anything she did to upset Him. I said, "TeTe, what could you ever do to upset Him? Take an extra cookie from the cookie jar?" Believe me when I tell you that TeTe was a saint. Her example and legacy of heartfelt consistent love makes me tear up even now. She will always be remembered as one of God's angels. Ask anyone. And yes, we all knew that we were blessed to have her in our lives.

There is an incident that occurred in the first two years of my forty-eight-year marriage to the Bear, as I call him. It is still etched in my mind as if it happened yesterday.

Tommy and I were stationed at Fort Leonard Wood, Missouri. Tommy was in the Jag Corps and occasionally came home for lunch. I was learning to cook. I was not talented in the kitchen; however, on this particular day, I had attempted biscuits, a most ambitious project for me. I was very excited at the prospects of surprising Tommy. He was to be home at noon, and I was ready.

It was twelve thirty, and Tommy came through the door with a smile and a hug. I was not receptive. I was covered in flour, and my biscuits were burned. I looked at Tommy before he could say a word and exclaimed, "How could you be so inconsiderate?" I was Mama. He looked baffled and apologized for his tardiness, saying he had a hearing that ran late. I continued with my rant; Tommy just listened. After a few minutes, I took a breath and waited for response. Tommy said, and in his gentle voice, "Grem, I'm sorry, it couldn't be helped. I'm sorry that you worked so hard and burned your biscuits." He paused and looked straight into my eyes and added, "Grem, you've said a lot. Are you finished?" I was stunned and just stood there. Tommy then added, "Grem, we can't talk to each other like this. We love each other, and tomorrow when you have forgotten everything you've said, I will remember."

I felt so small. He had apologized and said he loved me, that it couldn't be helped, and that he would remember my words.

I cried and hugged him, repeating, "I'm so sorry. I just wanted to surprise you, and I was so disappointed that I burned your lunch." Yes, I was disappointed in me, not Tommy, and the worst shame was that I had called him inconsiderate. Words are not forgotten. They go straight to our mental computers.

Words are important; they can be uplifting or destructive. We need to guard our negative thoughts because they can damage us and others, and they scar our souls. I learned that day in faraway Missouri how to fight. Better yet, how to express my feelings accurately. It was a profound epiphany for me.

Tommy taught me a most valuable lesson, and he did it with love. Only love heals. I have reflected on that teachable moment so many times in my life. I have asked myself why we project out instead of looking in. I have asked myself why we have to place blame instead of admitting that we are hurt. It would appear that we don't want to be vulnerable, and yet those moments can be the most loving and nurturing.

This would remain the most valuable lesson of my life. We teach and communicate successfully when we come from love and thoughtfulness. We cannot revoke our words; they must be loving, helpful, and hopeful.

Tommy was able to move beyond my attack and without judgment or counterattack. He saw a wife who wanted to surprise him, a wife trying to cook for him, and though my efforts were in vain and burned, he saw only love. We were never to mention this again, but I would never forget that there was no judgment of me or no retaliation. This is an important and profound moment in time. God was redirecting my learned behavior.

I would mention one other incident preceding this one to demonstrate the importance of humor in relationship, humor that I would often invoke when encountering Mom on difficult days for both of us.

Tommy was working on a case and said he would call me at eleven, a break in the court hearing. The call didn't come. I stewed and then decided I'd fix him! I would go to the ceramics shop.

I was remembering the army general who told me before leaving for Fort Leonard Wood, "I would leave a ceramics expert, a great bowler, or with a large family." Not too much to do at Fort Wood.

Tommy arrived home, and I was not there. I couldn't stay or wait and tell him that I was disappointed that he didn't or couldn't call; I would just leave. Was I petty? Yup, I was petty. I did not, at the time, have the tools in my box to say I was disappointed or hurt. To say this was to leave myself vulnerable. While I was stewing, I took it upon myself to say to me, "He just doesn't care." Where did that come from? You know.

I "poured" four Madonnas at the ceramic shop. It took a while, and then I headed back to 7 Delafield where I assumed Tommy was wondering where I was and what I was doing.

I pulled in the driveway in our brown station wagon with my four Madonnas in a box. Tommy was leaning over the back-porch railing. I put my window down and he said, quite innocently and with his contagious smile, "Hey, Grem, what did you make?" Wow! He wasn't concerned at all, but rather anxious to see what I had done at the ceramics shop. Total trust! Total innocence! Total love! He added, "Sorry I didn't call. We didn't get the anticipated break in the action. I'll carry your stuff in the house. Did you have fun?"

The truth was that I was game playing. I wanted him to know what it's like to anticipate a call from someone you love and not receive it. Circumstance didn't matter. Reason didn't figure in the situation. The only thing that mattered was my insecurity. Where did that come from? I never looked at it. I did that day, and I would always remember that because things don't always evolve the way we plan, it doesn't mean someone is conspiring to disappoint us. Things happen! It's as simple and complicated as that! I now had another new tool in my box—reason. And there was also the issue of self-esteem. Much to think about and all quite new to me.

The car is also extremely symbolic. The vehicle can, in dreams, represent our bodies that which moves us forward or backward in life, takes us to something or someone or away from it.

No doubt, that day at Fort Wood, I was running from me and my misguided computer of thoughts. That same brown station wagon brought me home to truth and to love.

PRRFEC ReVisited

My mom's car was her lifeline, her ticket to freedom, diversion, and private moments. When Dad passed, Mom wanted her car painted, wanted a new bumper, wanted the nicks and bumps repaired and covered. Tommy had this done for her.

She was on oxycodone and had cancer, which had moved to several parts of her body, and emanated from her head! And yes, she was driving every chance she could sneak out.

In years past, she and Dad had a home at Lake Gaston. She would occasionally drive down by herself and spend four and five days. She would drive to her daughters' homes and visit for a couple days now and then.

I remember her panic one morning when she went outside and found a flat tire on her auto. It was as if her whole world had fallen apart even though I told her Tom would fix it. She was inconsolable. I've pondered this many times. A flat tire is fixable and such a little thing in the scheme of things, almost insignificant to me.

The car was mom's freedom; it was important. She could talk about this Toyota a lot, commenting on its beauty and performance. Her life was somehow more perfect when she was alone and driving. Maybe that explains her license plate—PRRFEC. The car represented freedom and peace.

It was a source of confusion and sometimes inner conflict, for me, that she appeared uncomfortable when, through the years, Tommy had gifted me with a Cadillac convertible, Jaguar, BMWs, and a Porsche. I never asked for these surprises, but Tommy had worked exceptionally hard for a lifetime and loved, and still loves, surprising his family, all of us.

It has never mattered that these cars were fancy or not fancy. My children marvel at the fact that I drive slowly, don't use GPS, have never touched it, don't know or care that I have heated seats. I just want something that will get me where I'm going. I use only start, stop, forward, and backward. Believe it or not, it's true. What does matter is that I am loved and that my husband wants me safe. He cares.

Mama asked numerous times, "Why do you spend all his money?" "Why do you go around your elbow to get to your thumb?" "You waste Tommy's gas."

The simple truth is that I am geographically challenged. I go the only way I know; I do not like equipment and give it little or no importance in my life. I have examined my conscience many times. I have never sought material gain. I know I am blessed. I remember always the days I was teaching second grade while pregnant with morning sickness; I remember the first apartment and Tommy working three jobs while studying for the bar exam. I remember our first Christmas tree with three branches and the glittered pine cones we found in the woods and sprayed blue. I remember gifts given to each other with green stamps. I gave him a dartboard, he gave me a ballpoint pen. We'd play darts to see who changed diapers. We were ecstatically happy and in love.

Life has been good to us because of hard work and our love. We have had enormous tragedy with the loss of a child, and we know what matters and it's not stuff.

Stuff provides momentary joy. Love is forever with or without stuff. Thus, you know the source of my confusion with Mom's concerns.

Brave Souls

I do not want to deviate from caretaking; however, those who choose to support family in loving ways must also understand that it is an adventure not only into your past but also into your psyche and memories. It can be a thought-provoking examination of self on many levels.

We all have times in our lives when our cups are full. Sometimes, it seems that things are piled on and God is just waiting for us to cry *uncle*.

While we cannot eliminate sadness, tragedy, and stress in our lives, we can successfully move through it with the grace of God.

Think good thoughts. Summon each morning before putting your feet on the floor, your gift of joy. Trust me; it is there.

Count your blessings. We have so much to be grateful for. The fact that we wake up to a new day, a new opportunity is a blessing. Thank God for the day, the loving people in your life. Thank Him for the seasons, the sunrises, and the sunsets. Thank Him for His protection and for angels, ones with wings and those who walk the earth beside us. Thank Him for *time*; it's precious and a gift.

Look, as best you can, for balance in your life. You have to eat and something besides Cheetos and candy bars from hospital vending machine. Make time to eat breakfast and to energize yourself before venturing out. Our brains require nutrition to function properly.

Get a decent night's rest. Your disposition will thank you. It is amazing how much better we function with adequate rest.

As Mom's cancer became worse and one tumor grew and fractured her spine, her sleep was very interrupted. Often, she slept sitting up in a chair, tuning in and out to the TV for comfort.

I noticed a definite difference in attitude when she slept better.

Ask questions, but be patient and respectful. Don't overreact because you cannot function with clarity if you are coming from emotion. Don't be accusatory. Use your love and creativity to say things like, "Do you need more pain medication? Refresh my memory. How many do *we* take each day?" Use *we*; it takes the sting out of you.

What doesn't work? One example is, "Don't tell me you took five of these!" No one likes to be backed into a corner. Your goal is to get information in an unintimidating manner. Use "Are you OK?" Not "What were you doing?" or "I can't leave you alone for a minute."

Think in terms of how you would like someone to communicate with you. More helpful tips are knowing it's OK to have silences. I found, when I'd just sit, sometimes Mom would come out with a pearl. She might even have an opportunity to remember that call back from the doctor or the plumber or the telephone company.

Discreetly check for bills that might have been overlooked. Always remember there is great anxiety, fear, pain, anger, and depression.

It is a time for some bargaining with God. Unfortunately, we cannot crawl inside their heads and hearts and know all their thoughts.

I found it extremely important to ask each day, "Do you need or want anything?" I found it extremely important to check the refrigerator for eaten foods and out-of-date foods.

Mom loved to freeze everything. If she had no appetite, she froze it. Try to ask what would taste good and find it. Toward the end of Mom's journey, I found her tastes were all over the place. One day she wanted a chocolate chip cookie, another day she wanted a small milk shake, another day she was in the mood for broccoli.

At the journey's end, try as best you can to accommodate. Make your loved one comfortable, and comply as much as you can.

Sometimes, Mom didn't want to put her nightgown on. I believe there was also a fear of the long and painful nights when you are alone with your thoughts. If your mom, toward the end, wants to keep her clothes on at times, let her; respect her wishes. Pay careful attention to hygiene without being offensive. I would say, "Mama, I'm doing some laundry today. May I take that for you?" They are fragile and weak. Be very careful about lifting or moving them. Think in terms of a china doll.

Note that bathing is an enormous challenge. They deserve to be treated with the utmost dignity. "Mom, may I put a warm washrag on your neck? It always makes me feel better."

Remember that when we are stressed and cancer patients are stressed to the max, control kicks in and needs to be handled delicately. For the caretaker, I suggest taking a nice walk while noting the beauty around you, breathing deeply. Some have suggested, to me, eating pumpkin seeds. Physical activity is best.

For Mama, I would relate funny stories; laughter is therapeutic. It's also healing. Spinach and dark chocolate also dispel cortisol. Who doesn't love chocolate?

I have found that helping Mama was my gift to me. One smile from her was worth a thousand chastisements. There was enormous peace when she passed on because I knew, at the deepest level, that I had truly done everything I could.

The other factor that's interesting and the most significant is God's grace. Ask for it, pray for it, thank Him for it!

Initially, I would come home broken and feeling bad about myself. I felt inadequate. This is normal. As time went on, I ceased to hear criticisms and negativity. I would just laugh. That's God's grace, and it's available to all of us.

Something else that comes to mind and plagued Mama until the end was procrastination. This consumes all of us. This world assumes we always have tomorrow. We don't! I'm not attempting to be morbid, but all anyone of us has is *now*. I ponder the little boy in Richmond, Virginia, who went happily off to a Fourth of July celebration last summer. Imagine the family—excited, festively dressed, looking forward to fireworks and barbeque. Then someone carelessly shoots a gun in the air, and the little boy is killed. True story! Do you believe they thought they had tomorrow?

Mama knew for over six months that she had a place on her forehead that wasn't healing and was getting larger. She didn't want to look at it and kept increasing the size of her bandage.

I am confident that she felt, as a nurse, that something wasn't right. We encouraged her many times to see a dermatologist. Mom knew I'd had thirty squamous cell cancers removed. She knew I couldn't walk for four days due to pain and bandages on my feet. She knew I almost lost my finger to squamous cell cancer, but she refused to go to a doctor and refused to talk about it until Dr. Wornam removed a large portion of her scalp. This cancer is aggressive and spread and seeded in other places. It eventually took her life.

It is often a pain in the neck getting an appointment and sacrificing part of your day sitting in a doctor's office. What, however, is it worth? Your life? Please go. Please make the appointment.

I thought for a while that because she'd been a nurse and seen so much pain and sadness that she was afraid. I also thought that often we think if we don't focus on it, it will go away. It doesn't.

Don't procrastinate. If in doubt, see the doctor and put your mind at rest. Do it for yourself and those who love you.

One shocking thing I noticed taking Mom to radiation for two different sessions—one at St. Francis hospital and one at Johnston-Willis Hospital—was, once again, fear and loneliness. I couldn't believe that both young women and men as well as elderly men and women drove to radiation alone. There is no excuse for this with family, friends, and consoling church groups. Help is a phone call away.

Mom and I would befriend many while waiting our turn. One woman in her thirties had lost two sisters and her mother to breast cancer. She drove each day to radiation alone and then went to work forty minutes away. She commented she had to work and that her bills were astronomical.

Mom and I would talk to her, and I would bring little prayers and prayer medals to her. I believe Mom looked forward to seeing her. I also believe that it gave Mom some comfort speaking to her.

This was her second round of chemo and third round of radiation. Her chest was bloodred, and Mama noticed. Mom would talk about her to family and especially to me, saying, "I feel badly. She is much worse than I am."

I would contend that comforting or helping others makes us feel better about ourselves.

So look around. There's the man without shoes and then there's the man without feet.

Mom's radiation the second time around was rough. Because she had the tumor in her spine, the radiologist explained to me that the treatment for Mom would affect the tip of her stomach and that we would, most likely, deal with nausea and vomiting. We did.

Mama was very courageous, saying very little. I just wanted to hold her. Sometimes I did, but mostly she would not let you. I often wondered if I just continued to hold her I might open a floodgate of tears that would never stop.

I saw Mom tear up one day in radiation when she picked up a book of paintings done by cancer patients. She never talked about it, just gently put it back on the table. One artist had drawn a lonely dolphin spiraling upward out of the water. It was beautiful and brought tears to my eyes.

Please do not let the people you love or know go to radiation, chemo, or MRI alone. If you can't drive, find someone who can. For those with cancer in the spine or back area, as my mom, it is extremely painful to lie flat for CATs and MRIs. They need assistance, and they may not ask. Many, I have found, do not want to be a burden to caretakers. The gift you give is to yourself.

One thing Tommy and I found helpful was to hold Mom's foot for CATs and MRIs. I found it very comforting to have Tom hold my foot during long MRIs. It's kind of like Linus and his blanket, and you are not totally alone.

People often asked me what gift to give the elderly that would have meaning. I suggest hand lotion, stamps, pretty handkerchiefs, stationary, candy, a certificate for grocery store, or donate hours for driving. Ask what kind of music they like. Purchase a pretty CD. You can volunteer to come and clean for a couple of hours. (This must be done very diplomatically.)

I didn't realize until the end how weak Mom was. She skillfully hid it, but the last five days at home, we had to move her bed, and there was a treasure chest of cups and straws, all used. She was too weak to wash, too weak to walk around her home and clean, so like a small child, she just pushed things under the bed with her foot.

The other thing you can do is skillfully shield them from well-intentioned negative people. Patients are suffering and are dealing with enough. They deserve to be surrounded by helpful, hopeful, loving people.

Remembering Lessons Learned

I would use the tools in my box to prepare and sustain me throughout this journey. I would learn to love more, laugh more, retreat when necessary. I would finally process "let go and let God". I would smile at all the lessons I would have the opportunity to learn. I would smile at my failure and learn some humility. I would step back as God let me see that I had not yet mastered patience and might not in the near future. I would learn to love me with all my warts. I would celebrate and learn to thank God for my humanness. I would learn to lean on Him in difficult times, and I would learn that I can't fix anybody but me, and that's a full-time project that I'm attacking with joy, laughter, and peace because He is at the helm.

Thank you, Jesus, for the time and the opportunities to come closer to you, to learn the lessons you handpick for me. Thank you for letting me be your broom that you might lovingly, one day, take me in your arms and say, "Good sweeping, and I love you, faithful servant." Amen.

Afterthought

There is a wonderful and helpful booklet entitled *Gone from My Sight* by Barbara Karnes, RN, an award-winning hospice nurse. I highly recommend it to anyone who is involved with caretaking and terminal diagnosis.

She shares guidelines and signposts to look for at the end of life, being very specific right down to days and hours preceding death. She discusses mood changes, blood pressures, respiration irregularities, skin color changes, food and fluid intake, pulse increases and decreases, sleep patterns, and much more.

You may write to her at Barbara Karnes, PO Box 822139, Vancouver, WA, 98682.

About the Author

Ann Marie Hancock has retired from the glamorous life of a well-known television personality, model, and talk show host and resides in Midlothian, Virginia. Ann Marie has been happily married for over forty years to Thomas F. Hancock III. They have three children and four grandchildren. Her accomplishments include as follows:

- only woman speaker at First Papal Conference in America
- author of *Be a Light Miracle at Medjugorie* and *Wake Up, America*
- top television personality in Virginia
- Red Cross's Breath of Life Awardee for Devotion to Humanity
- awardee, American Academy of Pediatrics on behalf of the International Year of the Child
- past member of the International Platform Association for Select Speakers in the United States and Abroad
- first media recipient of the Virginia Rehabilitation Association Award

Ann Marie is available for lectures. For more information, please write to:

Ann Marie Hancock
PO Box 724
Midlothian, VA 23113